God's River
of Love

God's River of Love

by
Jacquie Heidamos

Cover and Interior Photographs
by
Jim Heidamos

Published by River Publications, Inc.
Suttons Bay, MI

Publisher's Cataloging-in-Publication Data
Heidamos, Jacquie

God's river of love / by Jacquie Heidamos. –Suttons Bay, MI : River Publications, Inc., 2003.

p. ; cm.

ISBN 0-9729404-0-5

1. Belief and doubt. 2. Philosophy.
I. Title.

BD215.H45 2003   2003092009
121.6—dc21   CIP

With appreciation to Leah Nicholson and Kelli Leader of the Jenkins Group, Inc., Traverse City, MI, and to interior designer Barbara Hodge.

Printed in the United States of America

07 06 05 04 03 * 5 4 3 2 1

CONTENTS

Snapshots from My Worldview

Filling in Some Details

More Pictures

An Update

Snapshots from My Worldview

A Circle of Friends

As I sit in the loft of our home where I do my writing, across from me on a round table is a clay candle holder. There are four Mayan human figures in a circle with their arms and hands encircling the shoulders and backs of those next to them, with a candle burning in the center. I read that as legend has it, the Mayans gathered around the fire to share stories that would strengthen one another's hearts and souls.

Within the past few years from somewhere the thought came to me, softly and gently, as if on the wings of a butterfly: Instead of us humans going through the very difficult struggle of trying to develop spiritually from the bottom up, why not turn the whole thing upside down? Why don't we all start out by being spirits who are each an individualized portion of God, with the opportunity of bringing our own unique version of divinity into our current-day world and everyday lives?

After I thought about this for a while my response was—why not? And so that is the starting point of the following series of snapshots, which together form an overall composite word-picture album.

> *My perspective is:*
> *basically each of us is spirit,*
> *a portion of God*
> *here, now.*

What I see happening in today's world is that many people are contributing fresh ideas that are interweaving with those of others, where a new human song and story are in the process of being sung and written. My purpose in *God's River of Love* is to add my voice to those of others.

Over a month ago, the first of these mini-essays seemed to arise quite spontaneously from a place deep inside myself, sometimes when I was reading what someone else had written, sometimes in the morning after a night of dreams, and at times when I was cooking or cleaning. It's like they were ready to come forth, and so I would take the time to write them down on yellow sheets of paper, to later word-process with the computer, and then put into a logical sequence at another time. They began last November 1998.

These writings are not just dictations from some inner source but include my assimilated translations from years of reading, thinking, relating, and experiencing. I see myself as fully responsible for how I have interpreted others' ideas over the years and how I have used them in my life in relationship with my own ideas. These writings also contain something beyond my own assimilations, expanded perspectives from regions I feel are vaster than my everyday world. And here again, I am fully responsible for how I have interpreted and translated them.

It is now early in January 1999. I intuitively know more mini-essays will continue to develop as I move through time. I feel like I'm starting on a new voyage of discovery. One of the things I see in today's world is that many of the cultural pyramid structures of power are beginning to crumble and re-form. Because of this, the unique value of each person is becoming clearer and more evident. So it is that I am writing about my worldview as one human being in a circle of friends who is sharing experiences and ideas with other human beings in a horizontal manner.

Just as I have been strengthened and empowered with what others have shared in their writings when they have carried their voices onto printed pages, I too am setting forth ideas, stories, and pictures in words that may strike strengthening and empowering chords within other people. This is the background from which these snapshots are emerging.

What Is a Worldview?

A worldview is a composite of all the perspectives one has formed about everything—going from the most cosmic beliefs to the smallest of details. Some parts of a person's worldview have more significance and weight in his or her life than others. The most active and vital portion could be thought of as the core of one's personal philosophy about life.

Oftentimes, a person uses portions of her or his belief, thought, and emotion structures automatically, with not much awareness of the process. At other times, there is more awareness of how one thinks about oneself, other people, other species, and life in general.

Each person's worldview is her or his own individual perspective of reality. It is from its overall and specific dynamics that one makes connections with others and coforms events with them. One's worldview and its various ingredients also serve as the filters through which the world is perceived, the searchlights and selectors for what is seen, and how it all is experienced. Therefore, perception is closely tied to a person's ways of thinking and overall worldview.

You may be asking at this point what gives me the right or authority to write a book about my worldview and why it might have significance to you. My answer is that with some success I have disengaged the essence of myself from much of the cultural programming I experienced in my childhood and throughout my life. Therefore, many portions of my world-view and my thoughts about life have been carefully chosen and selected in my adulthood. Mine is the story of one human being who has done a certain amount of repatterning and hence has a certain amount of freedom I didn't have in my earlier years.

When I was a child growing up in southern California in the late 1930s and 1940s, beginning about age seven I began to question the validity of some cultural agreements being presented to me as Truth and Reality. These questions continued throughout my growing-up years and into adulthood.

Then about three-and-a-half years after my first husband and I decided to end our almost twelve year marriage, I met Jim on May 8, 1970, in Palm Springs, California. To my way of thinking there are some events and meetings that contain enormous amounts of energy. This was one of those times for both of us. From the beginning, the electricity and chemical reactions between us were incredible and have continued to play out dynamically in various ways over the years.

We believe we found traveling companions in one another who were both searching for new designs and new ways of living our lives. We were officially and simply married in Palm Springs, California, on October 30, 1970. For us, our journey together has been both a love story and an adventure.

In southern California we lived a good life—a fast-paced one. When Jim moved from Michigan to join with me, he transferred his skills from being a sales and applications engineer to working in the newly emerging financial services industry. I was teaching second grade. I had always wanted to live at the beach, and within about a year we bought a lovely home there to house us all. At various times our extended family included my daughter, Jim's daughter, his grandmother, and a cat, along with periodic visits from other family members.

Life moved on. By the summer of 1975, Jim's daughter had gone back to live with her mother in Florida. His grandmother returned to her roots in Michigan, taking the cat with her. And my daughter had gone to Asia for three months after graduation from high school. When she returned, she would be going to college in northern California. We had sold our home at the beach the previous spring and were living in a rented townhouse nearby.

Jim and I spent seven weeks during that summer in the Caribbean, getting perspective about our lives. It was at that juncture we made the choice to primarily leave the money-making/money-spending world, freeing up some time, although Jim would continue working with some of his clientele for the next few years. The lives we had been living didn't make sense to us any longer. It was not an easy decision for me to make because I had lived in southern California ever since my parents and I came there from Illinois in 1938.

We moved to the foothills of the Sierra Nevada mountains in northern California in the early fall of 1975. It was there on three acres with a surrounding hundred-acre woods that we built a modest home, doing a lot of the work ourselves. We had chosen a convenient location that was private and also fairly close to town. Over time we added an organic garden, we then extensively expanded in 1980.

From 1976 to 1986, we did considerable exploring of the natural world, of the designs of our culture including its history, and of our own personal internalized cultural belief structures. Our primary motivation was to make more sense out of our lives. Throughout those years, we studied and wrote extensively about the world's belief systems and current worldwide conditions—economically, environmentally, socially, and psychologically.

The studies and writing we engaged in were the early stages of exploring our own worldviews and where they came from, seeing ourselves living our lives amidst the context of our society, both past and present. We began to see everyone this way all over the globe. Even though each person certainly is an individual, concurrently they are always living amidst the context of their particular place and time.

So it is, over the years Jim and I have been formulating and reformulating our personal philosophies. One of the lessons we have learned is that each of us uses internal pictures, thoughts, ideas, and emotions, forming patterns with which we construct and play out our life events. *We think, at basic levels, human beings are pattern makers and users.*

Emotions and Mental Processes

A conclusion I have drawn from my experiences as a member of our culture during the past thirty plus years is that emotions have been highlighted, while mental processes have been downplayed. To my mind, mental processes include the use of thoughts, beliefs, ideas, concepts, internal pictures, memories, attitudes, and imagination.

As I look back over my life, there was one period of time in the 1960s when I did focus on what I was internally feeling almost continuously, checking in with myself and asking, "What's happening at this moment?" It was an interesting project and process. I would experience an emotion and then give it a word. I felt and named love, anger, frustration, relief, joy, disappointment, excitement, resentment, happiness, sorrow, despair, hope, jealousy, envy, elation, sadness, anxiety, fear, rage, and general pain, along with more subtle internal messages. Certainly, increasing my conscious awareness in those ways was and is invaluable. And I learned that emotions that are allowed to flow forth do change.

But after a while, I realized something was sorely missing for me. I didn't want to live my life *just* as a series of emotional experiences and events. It was all too random and felt incomplete. I decided I also needed to add in my mental processes. For heavens sakes, why did I have a mind if I didn't use it?

As I began to be more aware of the intermingling of my thoughts and feelings, I formed a way of thinking that has held up well for me over time. *It isn't the rational mind that causes difficulties. It is usually the contents we have used and use to fill our minds that bring forth the problems we then experience.*

I think when the wave emerged in our culture in the 1960s to focus upon emotional feelings, the mental programs of many people had become so complicated and heavy that it was a great relief to just not think. Instead, we were being advised to seek out emotional experiences that brought us pleasure or some release from pain such as food, sex, music, adventure, alcohol, and drugs. But it is my experience and observation that the mental programs an individual has incorporated internally over the years do continue to have life, and it is a good idea to find out what they are and then to activate effective steps to change the contents of one's mind. I believe emotions often result from our thoughts and also intermingle with them.

Why would one want to go to the trouble of sorting out the contents of his or her mind? I did it in order to get more on the input side of the process, becoming more of the artist of my own life.

In simplified terms, thought patterns (patterns of thought) can be seen as the forms, frameworks, and containers we use to construct the events of our lives, while emotions are the fuel that give them energy.

Mixtures of Ingredients

How I think it all works is that each of us uses patterns of mental thoughts and ideas, of beliefs, of emotions, of internal images, of desire and intent to form major portions of our life experiences and events. I say major portions because we are usually in relationship with others who are also setting forth their patterns, which affect the events and experiences of our lives, as ours do theirs.

How do we acquire these patterns to start with? I think from the time we as spirit enter the culture we are born into, becoming spirit-people, we are automatically and internally programmed by those around us with mental pictures, words, attitudes, beliefs, emotions, and actions. They tell us who we are supposed to be and how to act because of our gender, our religion, our laws, procedures, and other cultural agreements. These programs become impregnated and internalized within each of us.

Then as we go through our lives, we automatically use this mixture of cultural patterns, interweaving it with our individual reactions to and interpretations of what we are experiencing. At each step along the way, we oftentimes accumulate more patterns that we add to our mix. Since others are using their mixtures too, we all mix our mixes in an energy dance of creativity.

When Jim and I moved to the Sierra foothills in the early fall of 1975 and built our home together, we became even more closely involved with one another's mixtures of patterns. All of this intermingling has been part of the love story and adventure we have been putting together and experiencing since we met, including many conflicts.

After studying and writing for a while about belief systems and current worldwide conditions, we agreed we needed to think about producing income over time. Therefore, we decided to write a book, summarizing and synthesizing what we were discovering. We saw ourselves as essentially like every person, living our lives in the same tide of time and events as everyone else. We eventually named our manuscript *Something Different*, the title coming out of a dream I experienced in later 1977. When I wrote about it the next morning, I stated that I wanted something different than the cultural experiences the dream event contained.

During the years we lived in the Sierra foothills, our home was paid for, we grew much of our own food, and our wants and needs were very simple. Hence, we had enough money to live on for several years. We chose to believe we were investing in ourselves and each other as we studied, wrote, and carefully spent the money we had earned and accumulated.

Over time we submitted our manuscript to publishers. Even though there was some interest, it didn't sell, and we were faced with the reality of needing to generate income in the next few years. We decided to sell our home, free up the money we had in it, and move to the Midwest, to what we termed "the heartland of America."

One of the vital lessons I learned in 1985 was that no matter how hard I tried to get things to turn out the way I wanted, we didn't sell our manuscript, and we couldn't stay there. It just wasn't working. Why not? Because, from my point of view, I wasn't attuned enough nor harmonized appropriately with my own overall purposes for being here. The message was absolutely clear to me—I needed to align myself differently. So I said, "I give" and began to seek an inner feeling of harmony that tells me I'm on course. At the time, even though I had an overall divine framework I lived my life within, I didn't have the personal divine partnership I now have—one I needed to seek, become aware of, and intimately involved with—in order to fill out what I was and am capable of being and becoming.

In February 1986 we moved to Michigan, to the state where Jim had lived until he joined me in southern California in 1970. With our golden retriever, Rusty, we settled into a home in a working-class neighborhood in a town near Jim's alma mater, Michigan State University. We lived there for almost three years while we studied and reworked our manuscript. Again we sub-mitted it, again there was some interest, and again it didn't sell. The time had come to move back into a direct money-making mode. My perspective of today is that we each needed more experiences and understandings. We had more to do. Speaking for myself, I'm certain I did.

We both became licensed in real estate, moving to a mid-sized community in southwest Michigan. When we came directly back into our culture, we felt we needed to use accepted cultural patterns of thinking, communicating, and acting in order to fit in. About the most expanded I felt I dared be with real estate

God's River of Love

clients was to use my intuition and frame it within a context of saying something like, "I think there's a bigger picture in play here." Nevertheless, translating one's vaster understandings into the day-to-day world of business and income-production is a dilemma for many people, including us.

Over time, with money we borrowed from our families, we were able to start our own business that eventually included residential and commercial real estate, insurance, investments, and retirement and estate planning. In late 1996, after my mother passed on, I left the business to pursue another direction that I will talk about in some detail later.

Then, when Jim's father became rapidly ill with pancreatic cancer and passed on August 4, 1998, we moved our lives and what had become Jim's business to Ann Arbor, Michigan, where his eighty-seven-year-old mother lived. Since she was so strongly attached to her home and surrounding land and insistent upon staying there, we decided to remove some stress from Jim's life and relocate to that area. It was evident to us that she needed his emotional and physical support and couldn't do it by herself. Jim is an only child. We both felt it was important for him to be near her in these later years of her life. And at the same time we added another human being as a center stage member who uses a mix of designs and patterns that interrelate with the mixes each of us sets forth.

16

Who/What Is the I?

My worldview of today does not include a random universe, as I had been culturally taught in scientific terms. Now, I believe there are God-given processes that are designed into the system, there for each of us to use. One such process is that each of us breathes "life" into the patterns we energize—whether they are our own originations, reactions, or interactions with others. Next, the question arises: Who/what is the I breathing life into the patterns we set forth for the content of our lives?

Culturally, most of us have been taught we are either a male or a female human being, and with that definition, from the beginning of our lives, has come forth much of what each of us has identified with as far as who we believe ourselves to be.

Added to one's gender and species identifications are racial beliefs, religious structures, ethnic affiliations, class and educational status, relationship roles, job ranking, and national allegiances— along with other differentiations such as age. In those terms, I am a middle-class, white, college-educated, sixty-six-year-old female, who is also a wife, mother, grandmother, United States citizen of English and mixed European heritage, and a Christian using Jesus' basic precepts as I understand them.

Many people seem to think of themselves as being their experiences, telling themselves such things as "I am sick," "I am sad," and "I am lonely." Now certainly as individualized portions of God, as spirit and spirit-people, I do think it is very important to be aware of one's experiences, which I believe to be feedback loops of information from which we can make new choices and changes as the basic selves we are. However, if one keeps telling oneself how badly one feels, this person can dig a potentially deeper hole for further experiences along those same lines.

For much of my life, the various cultural definitions of who I was said to be seemed too tight for me, even though they of course contained elements of truth. Nevertheless, it was like I was being put into enclosed structures, whereas I intuitively felt there was more to me and all of us than our culture was telling us there was.

Over twenty years ago it became essential for me to detach the essence of myself as much as possible from all my cultural programming, from my body, thoughts, and emotions, and from my past and future plans. One major method I have used has been meditation. I have tried many types. Currently, I set aside a time to do this each day, usually around 3:00 p.m. I lie back in my recliner, relaxing fully. Then if there are thoughts, ideas, pictures, or feelings that need to come forth, I make room for them to emerge. After a while, when it feels like I can meditate, I carefully start off by positioning myself with my basic identity as spirit, a portion of God interrelated with all spirit. (I choose to believe each of us is an individualized portion of God, but none of us is God-Itself. I think this is way too much responsibility and gets into a type of grandiosity.)

After positioning myself as spirit, I am easily open to thoughts, pictures, direct experiences, and silences—whatever is appropriate for me that day. This is an opportunity to experience and discover myself without being attached to nor identified with the contents of my mind, my emotions, or my body. I am easily seeking, open, and trusting of whatever comes forth. There are many times when I primarily feel a harmonizing, balancing, and restoring. On other occasions, what emerges seem to be revelations. I'm an observer when I watch my breath or thoughts as they move through my mind.

Some days I am guided throughout the process regarding what I should emphasize, or I have an intuitive sense about what to make significant. There are times when I am no longer focused in the physical realm, and later I come back to my familiar world. If I fall asleep, I just begin to meditate when I awaken.

I also write in my journal, "Dances and Dancers," most days, at no set time, where there is a free flow of thoughts, ideas, emotions, advice, and information, portions of which come forth from what I choose to believe is a divine partnership. This writing process helps me sort out my life and oftentimes provides amazingly practical and effective answers to challenging situations. Some days I write about dreams from the night before. My overall focus is upon seeking and receiving divine guidance as I write. I then do what I can to integrate the results into my day-to-day living.

Outside and Inside

As I evaluate my life and look at others' lives, I think our culture's scientific emphasis has focused us strongly upon our physical five sense experiences—sight, hearing, taste, smell, and touch—along with general physicalized sensations. We have been taught that what reality consists of is a material objective world out there that can be measured and relied upon.

Then there is the somewhat discredited inner world that has been becoming more legitimate in the past three decades: one's personal dimension of dream experiences, imagination, inner pictures, inner voices, inner sensing, intuition, direct knowing, and spirituality in general. I also place thoughts and emotions into the category of these interior personal processes.

I have discovered over the years that in order to become knowledgeable about what goes on inside myself, I have needed to take the time to explore each of the internal senses, magnifying one or the other for a while in order to become more aware and proficient at understanding the messages I perceive. As an example, for almost a year in the late 1970s, I met once a week with my down-to-earth friend, Karen, for about three hours. We silently sent mental images and word messages to one another, writing down what happened during the process and some of our thoughts in subsequent discussions. We learned a lot, both of us becoming much more skillful with attuning to and interpreting our own inner sensing.

From my point of view, along with a five-sense world of communication through verbal and written language, there are inner channels of communication amongst ourselves as human beings and with members of other species.

After my mother passed on in October 1996, with the inheritance I received I felt justified to heed the call of my spirit to leave the business Jim and I had built. I used the opportunity of newfound time to do more inner explorations and to update myself regarding some of Jim's and my previous studies. I also completed the initial stages of writing a novel, but those plans had to be shelved when Jim's father passed on in 1998 and we moved across the state to Ann Arbor. As events unfolded, in order for me to continue being in harmony with the larger sweep of my life, it became obvious that moving was the appropriate thing for us and me to do.

The move made it necessary to rethink what I was doing. In order to finish the novel I was envisioning, I felt I would have needed the support network I had in place in our previous location. Then, it wasn't long after we were settled in our new home that these snapshots began to appear as described in "A Circle of Friends."

Where I have come to now, with my own version of personal potency, is to focus upon being aware and present at each moment in both inner and outer ways. However, there are occasions when I predominately choose one or the other emphasis—outside or inside. One of my intentions has been to become increasingly skillful at knowing when to do what, how, and where, along with blending it all harmoniously. I've also been learning how to ebb and flow more with the rhythms of my life, when at times I purposely let everything go.

America in the 1950s:
the Good Old Days?

Currently, I am hearing some nostalgia about the decade of the 1950s in the United States. That was the era when I was a young adult. I was born in October 1932 in Illinois, and my parents and I moved to southern California in 1938. In January 1953 I graduated from college with a teaching credential, married for the first time in December 1954, and became a mother in October 1957. For me, those times included quite a bit of predictability and restraint, which together provided a certain amount of security, but also generated feelings of discontent.

Looking back to those years, we all had far fewer choices for everything, making our lives simpler than those of today. This probably accounts for some of the wistfulness people now sometimes feel about that decade, especially during the times when their lives seem overly stressed and complicated.

The cultural patterns in use in the 1950s were such that most females in my generation were programmed to be wives, mothers, and homemakers. Many of us who went to college were guided into professions or occupations where we could work until marriage or could use our work skills for support later in life, "in case something happens to your husband." Some of the main choices for female jobs in that era were nursing, teaching, or secretarial work. My own choice was between teaching and commercial art, with teaching winning out.

Having fewer choices also included the overall belief structures within which we lived our lives for what was said to be Reality. By the time I was in my teens in the 1940s, I experienced our culture as being quite unanimous in agreement about certain aspects of human nature and the roles for males and females. As I see those times from my perspective of today, one of the agreed-upon beliefs was that we humans were basically tainted in some way or another. Therefore, there was the need to oftentimes control or repress one's human nature, especially sexually.

The cultural revolution that came about in the United States in the 1960s and 1970s certainly did open things up! One of the mantras of the times by the youth was to "never trust anyone over thirty." To a considerable extent, the younger people were throwing out the past as they attempted to bring about a better present and future.

Prior to the 1960s, my generation was still responding to the Depression of the 1930s and World War II in the 1940s. Although the Western powers had stopped Nazi Germany and Japan, the prices had been high in terms of lives and time lost. The young men I knew and have read about who came back to the United States from World War II were definitely not carefree. Most of them had matured considerably and were very clear about their priorities. After the war many of them felt an urgency to carve out their place in American society, and many of them went to college on the GI Bill, during which time some of them married and started families. This was still the era when the males were expected to support their wives and children.

My first husband was seven-and-a-half years older than I was. He had turned eighteen in early 1943 and had been sent over to Europe with the U.S. Army. He was completing his last year of professional training at the time we were married.

I think one of the reasons money and material things were so important to us as adults in those post World War ll years was because most of us had little when we were children and teenagers. After the scarcities during the Depression, there were still scarcities during World War II when U.S. industry was mobilized for the war effort and almost everything was rationed.

Contrasting the character and values of the people from the 1930s, 1940s, and 1950s with the present, what do I see? *In the 1930s, 1940s, and 1950s we lived within a different context than we do now.*

In addition to having far fewer choices in all ways than one has today, life was more easily divided into right and wrong. It was clear to almost everyone during the Depression era that doing without jobs, enough money, and enough food was not right. When I was a young child, my father was without a steady job for about three years, doing pickup work when he could, while my mother worked at a department store. There were occasions when my parents were still hungry after dinner, but they made sure I wasn't.

It was also easier in those earlier decades to be patriotic. It became clear to almost everybody in the United States after a while that what Hitler was doing in Germany was wrong and had to be stopped, especially after the Japanese bombed Pearl Harbor. As I remember it, during World War II we Americans were united as a country in the war effort, breathing a huge sigh of relief when the war was over and war industries were shifted into peacetime activities. This unity of purpose is in stark contrast to what happened later in the United States during the Vietnam War.

My sense today is that the generation who became adults during World War II had experienced enough excitement and drama in their lives, and we of the following generation were hugely affected by the early events of *our* lives—the Depression and World War II.

I am speaking from the position of having been a member of the white middle class, even though in my childhood it was the lower middle class, in my teens the middle middle class, and then in my adulthood the upper middle class. My first direct awareness of some of the racial problems that were part of the American story was when my Japanese friend from second grade and her family were later sent to an internment camp during World War II. On a wall in the loft that is both my writing room and what I call my "nest," there is a picture of my second grade class. I look happy and relaxed. I see my Japanese friend with a quizzical, questioning look as if saying, "What's going on here?"

Below the surface of prosperity and tranquillity in the 1950s were undercurrents in America that eventually surfaced, actually starting in the 1950s, then becoming more widespread and dramatic in the 1960s and 1970s. One of these was from some of us females who had been feeling way too confined by the cultural roles we had been playing. Another was from many young people who felt way too confined by the content of their schooling, where patterns from the past were being unquestioningly passed on to them. Blacks began to demand humane treatment and a fairer playing field. Homosexuals began to speak out for recognition and respect. And during the Vietnam War, Americans were bitterly divided over whether we should even be there in the first place.

During my first marriage, by the early 1960s I felt like my life had become a series of roles—wife, mother, cook, nurse, shopper, show piece, and sex partner. I somehow felt in danger of losing myself. Where was I amidst all these expectations and activities? The situation I found myself in was quite strange for me because in my childhood and adolescence I had a strong sense of myself. Returning to teaching in early 1963, after our daughter had been in kindergarten half the year, helped somewhat.

By the late summer of 1966, when I was thirty-three, one day while taking a shower, in despair I told myself I was perfectly miserable, even though I had done and achieved just about every-thing my culture said I should for a good life. This included having a handsome husband with a successful professional career, a lovely home, a beautiful child, cars, clothes, and a professional career of my own. I often felt like I was trapped in a rectangular box, going back and forth in the space between the walls.

We had begun our marriage December 18, 1954, and we separated in November 1966, almost twelve years later. As I understand it today, what had connected the two of us in the first place, and held us together over the years, had been replaced by our differing desires for where each of us wanted to take our lives.

Over time, the very deep knowing which had been within me for most of my life—that there was more to life than our culture was telling us there was—would grow and grow, as would the certainty that if I just kept seeking it, I could and would find this "more."

I can now see the search for my fundamental identity was a rather nebulous theme, that was an undercurrent and pressure in my life, that surfaced directly during the 1970s.

Do I think, as a society, we are currently better off than we were in the 1950s? In many ways I do. Even though today's environment is more complex with the increased numbers of options, along with fewer behavior restraints and more competition, there is also more personal freedom. In addition, we are living in an interconnected global society, which includes worldwide communications and information. Added to this is the whole generalized spiritual quest that seems to be accelerating.

Jim and I recently saw the movie *Pleasantville*, which contrasted some of today's attitudes and customs with those of our early adult years. On the way home I remarked, "What was seriously missing in those earlier times for me was my understanding of the matrix of divinity I now know I have always lived my life within," to which Jim wholeheartedly agreed. He said, "It was there all the time. I just didn't focus on it."

Being Human

In general, as I understood it, the main cultural agreement about what a human being is when I was growing up in the Los Angeles, California area was hugely influenced by the scientific perspective of the times. The scientific viewpoint I learned was that all of life evolved from the random coming together long ago of various components that resulted in what has been called the Big Bang, where human beings were seen to be the most advanced species in a long chain of evolutionary development, as a result of survival of the fittest.

It was believed we humans were limited to our five senses within our scientifically described human bodies in time and space. And if there was more—a sixth sense, an intuition or gut feeling—it was said to have come about from what had been experienced before in one's life and was stored in one's unconscious to be called upon to help one in the present and future.

As I grew up, I also learned that many in the scientific community believed that if a person held religious beliefs, they were weak or neurotic, where needing religion was seen as a crutch.

Now, if the beliefs I have just described are a person's starting point for what it means to be a human being, I think life is a scary and lonely reality. This composite helps me understand why someone with that worldview could decide to have as many material possessions and experiences as possible, because this life is quite probably all there is. For some people, included in this way of thinking is the assumption it is a dog-eat-dog world, which is one way we humans can see ourselves and others.

Another viewpoint in my growing-up years was the one I heard in various Protestant Sunday schools and churches I attended. I learned we humans were created by God. We were His children, but He was a strict Father who expected obedience. He was up there watching each of us but was outside of ourselves as human beings. God was said to be perfect; we humans were imperfect. Because of Adam and Eve's actions, we all were tainted from birth, with tendencies for both good and evil. Therefore, we had to be watched closely and couldn't be trusted too far, both as individuals and as a species.

Jim grew up in the Midwest. In his experience, the combination of the belief of God being the Creator of everything and the Adam and Eve story became the starting point for what a human being was said to be. As Jim remembers it, most of the scientists he knew believed the Old Testament Biblical stories to some extent, mixing together the scientific viewpoint with the Biblical one.

And yet another picture came forth for me as a child and an adolescent, both from the churches I attended and from my own reading of the New Testament, especially Jesus' words and actions: God is Loving, and as human beings that's what we all needed to focus on—God's love for each of us, our love of God, and our love for one another. We humans could and should somehow fill ourselves and our lives with this love.

I suspect I wasn't the only one who carried around versions of these various belief constructions in those years, beliefs that certainly didn't all harmonize with one another! But in those earlier times I had no way to articulate what was happening, and even if I had, who would I have talked to?

Being human? My current-day way of thinking about human beings is that throughout our history we have used many maps, different pattern combinations out of which we have lived our lives.

My choice now is to think about each of us first as spirit, a part of God, with our own portion of God that is vitally interested in us and our lives. At the same time, how I think it works is each of us, as spirit and a spirit-person, has free will to use and energize whatever version of being human he or she chooses, whether purposely or automatically due to previous programming.

Furthermore, I think in order to be open to divine input and direct help, she or he needs to seek it and be attuned to its messages.

There are more than likely multiple versions of ourselves available for each of us to fill out in our lives. The one I continue to choose is the most filled-out version of me there is, in an empowered divine sense, whatever it is. I mentally turn a kaleidoscope until the wholest me comes into focus, to which I say, "That one!" This becomes a guiding light for me to use. *I also believe there is no stopping point in terms of evolvement—when a person reaches one place, there is always more to become, in a joyful sense.*

Love Is a Many-Splendored Thing

Oh my, all the ink, all the thoughts, feelings, and actions that have been set forth in the name of love! And rightly so, I say, because I believe Love in its originating form is primarily what brings about our world and our lives within it.

When I first saw the film *Love Is a Many-Splendored Thing* in 1955, I was strongly affected by it. Since then, I have seen it a number of times, the most recent being last night on a television channel specializing in old movies. Looking back on my life, it seems to me there were images from it I somehow unconsciously carried within myself, from the first time I saw it, that were reinforced with subsequent viewings.

What had impacted me was what I perceived to be the depth and breadth of love between the woman and the man, while at the same time each one was an independent, productive person. As a female I especially liked the role Jennifer Jones played as an intelligent, compassionate physician, an equal in her own way to any man. She was a Eurasian doctor, and William Holden played the part of an American reporter. The setting was Hong Kong.

One night, not long after I met Jim in 1970, I dreamed about us. In my dream I saw him coming up a hill to where I was standing. He was wearing hiking clothes and using a walking stick. I think this was my version of some of the hilltop scenes from the 1955 film. It was also a message to me that this was more than likely a connection I had been bringing about for years! When Jim and I moved to northern California in 1975, the picture in my dream played out in our lives in terms of doing a lot of hiking and backpacking together in the Sierra Nevada mountains, as well as the degree of love we have oftentimes shared.

For many years now I have believed a level of divine love has vitally connected Jim and me, flowing between us even before our first meeting. I also think this underlying love became obscured at times due to many of the cultural patterns each of us had ingested in our past, through which we funneled this creative power of divinity we culturally call love. In addition, our lives became filled with our jobs and other people, including their mixes of patterns. That was what happened to the characters in the film, too.

Recently, I think Jim and I both have reached a place where we are able to more consistently experience the multiple facets and delights of divine love—our love for God and Its love for us, our divine love for our own selves, our love for each other, and our growing love for everyone and everything. Included in all of this for me has been an ever-increasing divine trust.

Divinely loving ourselves has taken a considerable focus by both of us in recent years, primarily because of our cultural programming that taught us loving oneself was selfish. For me, added to this was my cultural gender indoctrination that told me my role as a female was to care for others, from where my rewards were supposed to come. At present, I think selfishness comes about when one is afraid there is not enough to go around and one has to fight for what she or he wants, whereas divine self-love is both wise and generous to all, which most certainly includes oneself.

I believe a person operates on a different wavelength when he or she predominately uses fear, as compared with the wavelength one operates within when one predominately uses divine love. My experiences and observations are that fear entraps and encloses, whereas divine love is open and expanding.

This morning just before awakening, I experienced a dream in which I was in a rectangular-shaped store of sorts, with men who didn't have my best interests in mind. There were floor-to-ceiling shelves of food items everywhere, many in boxes. The doorway to the outside was also filled with shelves and food, camouflaging the opening. When I felt fear everywhere in the store, I burst through the doorway area. It proved to be one-dimensional, like heavy paper.

Later, when I contemplated the dream, I saw that the fears one can feed upon are everywhere in our culture, like the food in the store. And when one is within those fear enclosures, one doesn't even necessarily know there is somewhere else to be.

For me divine love is not the polarity of fear but instead is the foundation and overall framework within which each of us fundamentally lives our lives. I've been on a personal quest for years now to discover its components.

A Current-Day Myth

One night a few years ago, I experienced a dream so dynamic I got up around 3:00 a.m. to write about it. It took place within a fertile mental and emotional soil, when I had been thinking about how much energy was being put into searching the past for myths that would somehow apply to our lives of today. I had reached the conclusion that even though those of the past certainly had value, each one primarily belonged to another time and place, amidst a culture different than ours of the present.

Therefore, when this dream occurred, I could easily interpret it as a current-day myth, even though its setting had a more primitive feeling about it. I could see how it could help people of today question their priorities and focus more clearly upon what really matters in their lives.

The dream came forth in the later months of 1996 when I was being divinely advised to move out of my business activities with Jim and begin preliminary preparations to write a novel. After I thought about it for a while, I could see how I could use the mysterious appearance of a myth into a Midwestern American community as part of the novel's central theme, in terms of how it affected people's lives and how it connected them with one another. It was clear I should purposely keep the story plain, allowing readers to more easily project their own images into it, where they also could use their imaginations to add to it in other ways.

This is the myth I interpreted from my dream and had intended to use in the novel I was putting together, which I set aside due to the passing on of Jim's father and our move to Ann Arbor.

The River of Love

So it is that somewhere in time and space a woman goes daily to a river, for comprehensive understandings and nourishment.

She immerses herself within its waters, going to a depth and place of life that is outside the usual limitations of her five-sense experiences.

She rests and restores there.

And she learns lessons she needs to learn.

Along with love, strength and power are part of the river, which flows within her, too.

But at first when she came back to the village and talked about what she was learning, the people were afraid. They had been told all sorts of terrible things could happen to them if they went to the river. "No. No. No," they said. "This life isn't great, but it could be a lot worse."

And so it was that they continued to do what they had been doing, but they increased their pace and amount of activities. They were going faster and faster.

Then, after a while some of the villagers began to grow weary and become restless. They started questioning, saying to themselves, "Surely there must be more to life than this."

Slowly, a few people began to go to the river, to find out first-hand what was there.

Now it is true, along the way to the river some of them did meet unpleasant creatures who tried to keep them from their destination. But those who went on to the river discovered they too were rested, restored, nourished, and were gaining comprehensive understandings that they could use in their lives and talk about with other people.

The adventurers who went daily to the river of love began to live differently. Slowly, they began to restructure their priorities. Many of them found themselves pausing during the day to listen to a bird sing, to enjoy the feeling of the wind stroking their bodies, and to smile in appreciation of their fellow villagers.

Many of them learned that in the river it is usually unnecessary to make most of the choices they had been making between this and that. They began to look for ways to weave elements together they had never tried to blend before. Rather than debating two sides to questions as they had in the past, they sought to include the best ideas from all the people. They were discovering and applying some aspects of basic wisdom and common sense the river was showing them.

More and more people began to go to the river, and they too sometimes met creatures along the way who tried to keep them from their destinations, but those who got there were also rested, restored, and nourished. They too were gaining comprehensive understandings within the river that they could use in their lives and could talk about with others. And they, too, began to shift.

In the river, each person's daily experiences were different from those of the others, and as they shared their stories, it happened naturally that there was an increased appreciation for the value and uniqueness of each of them.

Over time, it also happened naturally that they could see each person had special abilities and skills which could enrich their village. This was such a delicious way to think and to live life, it took them awhile to realize how much they all had changed. Rather than trying to limit others because of the fear of what they would do, they were encouraging one another to be as full and whole as they could be. Their lives began to have a depth and breadth they hadn't known before, and they were able to appreciate their uncultured spirits.

A momentum developed. Even though each person had to face her or his issues and fears—the unpleasant creatures who stood in the way—it was wonderful to be able to talk with others who were also dealing with their issues and fears. As they told their stories, there were frequently sighs of recognition— there were similar themes for many of them. At times they laughed, wept, sang, and danced together.

What freedom they felt! Freedom from uncomfortable and disabling ways of living their lives. Freedom to feel good about themselves and each other. They realized people had done what they had done or not done in the past because they had been entrapped in a belief enclosure, one that had included them all in certain ways. And they said, "It's O.K. to feel anger, sadness, grief, and pain, knowing one can move beyond them now."

Everyone found a type of nourishment in the river of love. In the past, nourishing and nurturing had been given to the females to express. That was just the way it had been. But as more and more men experienced basic nurturing from the river, many of them began to funnel what they were learning into their male ways of doing things. They were beginning to be able to nurture themselves, women, children, and other males. They began to be gentler people.

Men were also being freed to listen to women as fellow human beings and to find them interesting from that perspective. Their male egos were changing.

The sacred and divine were now being interwoven throughout people's daily activities and experiences as contrasted with only being emphasized on special occasions.

From their daily trips to the river, some saw how they had been using ways of thinking and acting because that's what they had been taught by their parents and the rest of the villagers who had been taught those same things by their parents and the rest of the villagers who had been taught by their parents and the rest of the villagers who had ...

Many of them burst out laughing when they realized how seriously they had lived out the accepted teachings, and how fiercely they had fought to defend them or to rebel against them.

Numbers of men who went to the river understood over time that they had used a type of power in their lives—power that directed and dictated—while in the river they experienced power and strength in its basic form before it was funneled into various human-devised patterns. Even some of the most aggressive males began to free themselves from their previous ways of doing things, the result being their lives became a lot more joyous.

Fatherhood also changed because eventually their patriarchal society just naturally had been dissolving as they implemented their new understandings.

Each person was easily expected to be a responsible human being, according to their age and maturity. People were responsible in different ways now, each within a framework of fairness, appropriateness, and individuality. Relationships became much more enjoyable between males and females, between parents and children, and between people of all ages.

The river was teaching each person who went there what he or she needed to learn. Within the river of love, many people were acquiring specific skills to help them live their lives in ways that were healthier, fuller, and more whole. And as people became more skillful and more expanded, anger, rage, resentment, and envy decreased measurably.

Women learned in the river of love about some of the patterns they had been automatically using as females, through which they had funneled basic love, leading themselves into undesirable alliances. Then they were able to replace the unhealthy patterns with those that brought them more enriching experiences and interactions.

In the river, many people learned in their own unique way about some of the basics of life, such as the need each person has for the flow of caring connections with others. And they learned how basic guilt naturally arose when the need for the giving and receiving of caring and positive involvement was violated.

Over time the use of alcohol and drugs for escape decreased because people no longer had to run away from themselves and the lives they were living.

In the river they learned there is a basic need for the sacred and the divine built within each human, so therefore each person began to construct his or her life along those lines.

Many also learned how miraculous their bodies really are, how each individual body is equipped with healing mechanisms that could be activated with the appropriate attitudes, beliefs, and activities.

The river was a gentle teacher, and the people were eager students. Something everyone learned is that the river of love flows within each person, deep down beneath her or his social programming and gender orientations. And all one had to do was to go there.

And so it is that somewhere in time and space, a woman, a man, a boy, a girl, and many other people each day go deeply within themselves to the river of love for comprehensive under-standings and nourishment. They rest and restore there. And each one learns lessons she or he needs to absorb and apply.

Yes, the lives of the people are good, and they are getting increasingly better.

The Past Is Oftentimes Alive

From the earlier days of what is now called the United States of America, people who came to this land voluntarily from elsewhere usually came for the purpose of living a better life than the one they had been experiencing before. They were seeking freedom from oppression and numerous other opportunities.

The exceptions were black slaves who were brought here from Africa and those white immigrants who crossed the Atlantic and arrived here in chains as prisoners, indentured servants, or bonded laborers. I read that large numbers of people—including poor or abandoned children—were kidnapped off the streets of London and other big cities and then sold to ship captains who transported them to the American colonies. They were then resold as laborers to the highest bidder, although between a third to a half are said to have died on some voyages. A similar thing happened on black slave ships.

Nevertheless, from the time of the Europeanization of this land, the majority of the people have been actively focused on the present and future. This has brought about a vital, youthful, energetic nation of inventors, entrepreneurs, explorers, adventurers, pioneers, and dreamers.

As I perceive it, the United States of America has been filled with feelings of hope and optimism that come about when one is able to open up new vistas and horizons. Going across the continent to the West, mapping uncharted territories (for them), became a lure for the early explorers and pioneers, whereas, in today's world our country is criss-crossed from sea to shining sea with networks of highways for our nation's cars and trucks. The skies overhead are filled with airplanes connecting people to places all over the continent and world. And not only do we have labor-saving devices in our homes and industries, we also now have microchips, computers, and the worldwide Web. Certainly we Americans haven't developed everything, but I think we have done a lot!

The picture I see is one of our nation having a history of optimistic forward-thinking that has brought about physically comfortable lives for many of us. Nevertheless, the down side, if one chooses to think that way, is that we Americans have been so busy with the present and future that we haven't taken much time to understand the dynamics of the past, which I believe have been and are operating today in our society.

Not only do I think the past frequently continues to be active culturally, I also believe the same process has been taking place within each of us—where in certain ways the patterns of our individual pasts continue to operate.

Recently, I've been quite fascinated to watch audience members from the Oprah Winfrey daytime television program, with guest professional help, be able to connect their current-day circumstances back to experiences and attitudes they formed early in their childhoods. They had not consciously realized that these earlier patterns were defining large amounts of their lives, such as how much money they had in the present and why they were having problems with their male/female relationships. From the memories that came to them almost immediately when they were guided to go back to the past, each one was able to make the connections between their earlier times and their life of today. My personal opinion is that what each of them brought forth is a small portion of what each of us carries around inside ourselves.

The professionals I saw on the Oprah programs showed how once a person remembers previous events, experiencing the feelings connected with them in the present, a new way of thinking can begin. I also would describe this as a process of changing the contents of one's mind, including associated emotions, by removing an old pattern and inserting a fresh replacement to use for one's life.

The process of pattern replacement I have been using is to first identify what the problem-causing pattern is. Then I take the time to kick back and relax for a while, where I imaginatively see the pattern as part of my inner contents. Next, I mentally remove or dissolve it, literally picturing that happening. I replace it with a new pattern if it seems to be the appropriate thing to do, although sometimes I leave an open space. Over time, if I discover the old one is still operating, I continue the above process until it is removed. There have been a few patterns I was unable to eliminate, and I have learned they were there for reasons I would discover over time.

When I first started this procedure over two decades ago, I kept track of the restructuring I was doing in my journal. Then I would follow up to see how my life experiences changed over time. One result was that many kinds of difficult events just didn't occur any more!

In addition, I have found it *very* helpful to sit down and write about an issue or theme. I trace it from the beginning of my life to the present for the purpose of seeing the whole sweep clearly, in order to have a current-day perspective of where I've been and where I am now. Then I can reflect upon what I have written.

One of the biggest gifts I have learned to give myself is that when I've done something I'm not happy about in my life, I forgive myself. I don't whitewash it; I learn from it, translating my understandings into new choices.

A significant problem that I think has taken place here in the United States since the 1960s is even though many of the cultural agreements were overthrown and new ones were introduced, the old ones still live on in customs, institutions, expectations, attitudes, and the individual interior programs each person already has. So for some people, what has happened is that they added another set of designs to the old ones, where, as I see it, they all intermix together. When I reflect about this picture for a moment, my reaction is—no wonder it's such a confusing world today, and no wonder there are those who want to go back to an earlier time and just use the patterns from that era!

Can we go back? I don't think we can. I think the only choice we have is to move ahead.

The Future

Certain people—whose ideas I have been hearing on television or reading in print—are saying there is going to be a type of worldwide disaster in the future. They see that forecast as the way it will all turn out, or at least as a potential they are unable to stop as we move toward the calendar year 2000 and a new century.

In the Christian religion there have been and are those who think John's vision in the book of Revelation in the New Testament was a God-given future blueprint. My perspective is that it was a dramatic picture John saw of what could happen if some of the large-scale patterns in use in his day were continued to be played out into the future.

I believe all future forecasts are probabilities that are flexible and can be changed if the appropriate efforts are put forth to do so.

From my point of view, when someone believes a future catastrophe is inevitable, she or he gives her or his own creative fuel to that *probability*. As a contrast and as another choice, if someone believes there are multiple probabilities that can be chosen and experienced around a situation, then that is a different matter. *I believe results come about from what we as individuals choose and focus upon, which then becomes a critical mass of group energy.*

I recognize there may be some members of the human species who would like to experience the excitement and drama of a worldwide event of cataclysmic proportions such as a nuclear world war or an environmental breakdown. It certainly is their right to make those kinds of choices. I also think most people believe they are helpless in the face of such probable disasters, with no other recourse than to pray they won't happen.

As previously stated, my picture of how it all works is that each of us has God-given powers we use all the time to fashion our lives in relationship with others who are doing similar things. And most certainly prayer is helpful! Therefore, my choice is to focus my thoughts and energies in order to bring forth a present and future in which I apply the lessons of the past in positive ways, as best I can for all of us, from the position of being an empowered spirit and spirit-person. I see this as an interesting, exciting, and desirable probability, and I invite others to send forth their own energies to make it our actuality and reality.

Nevertheless, I *know* that if we blow up our world or destroy it environmentally, we-as-spirit go on ....

Divine Guidance

The first time I was directly aware of a particular kind of deeper dimension within myself was one day in 1966. Over the years, I have come to know it as divine guidance from my personal portion of God. The event took place when I was taking a shower, while telling myself I had done everything I had been taught to do by my culture—and I was perfectly miserable! Then an inner voice that was not my own, and I didn't hear with my physical ears, calmly and steadily said, "Take a creative leap." I-as-Jacquie said to the other presence, "Yeah. What am I supposed to do, leap into the void?" The voice again said, "Take a creative leap," and it continued to give me the same advice repeatedly during the next period of time. Shortly afterward, my husband and I dissolved our almost twelve-year marriage—with mutual consent.

During my growing-up years and on into my adulthood, the cultural consensus about normality as I understood it came out of beliefs that stated emphatically the physical world one experienced with one's five senses was the whole of Reality. Usually, anything beyond that was said to be weird, abnormal, or crazy. Therefore, I became one of many people in those days who experienced some of the "more" to my life and didn't tell anyone about it. In my opinion, within the context of those times, it was just good sense to keep this type of experience to myself.

Oftentimes my divine guidance has been simple, direct, and repetitive. In 1974 and 1975, when Jim and I were still living in southern California, I was driving the freeway daily from our home at the beach to an inland community where I taught second grade. For months during my drive in the morning, I heard inner guidance say, "What you need, honey, are 10 ccs of courage to be your being the way you need to be, to do what you need to do." And so for months I would imaginatively give myself a shot of courage—over and over again. Did it work? I think so.

After we moved to northern California, there were many days, as I jogged along a path in the woods, I inwardly heard, "What's so bad about feeling good? What's so bad about feeling good?" It was like a continuous chant. This alerted me to take a look at the results of some of our cultural programs, where one oftentimes feels bad and does not feel good, and to do something about the inner tapes I had along those lines.

About a year-and-a-half ago I inwardly heard, "Open the whole thing up." So I did. But when I kept on hearing the same words I questioned, "More?" "Yes," it seemed to be saying. "More and more and still more. Open the whole thing up."

To my recollection, a back and forth dialogue with this inner voice of divine guidance began in the fall of 1996, right after my mother passed on. This was the time when I experienced direct knowing that I needed to move out of the business world and pick up on past mental, psychological, and spiritual explorations that I had begun in the later 1970s, when Jim and I lived in northern California. As I mentioned earlier, the fall of 1996 was also when I *knew* I should begin preparations to write a novel that would have *The River of Love* myth as its central organizing theme.

After I made the move out of our business life in the later months of 1996, I heard an inner voice ask me if I was prepared to go where all this took me. Was I prepared to live my life following divine guidance on a day-by-day basis—and just do that? Could I do what I would be doing with preparations for a novel, without assurance that there would be a product—a book—at the end? Could I be a person who would graciously and with no reservation accept the result of this forthcoming journey, whatever it was—anywhere from nothing visible to great fame, or somewhere in between? I answered yes to all the questions. I knew why I had been asked about fame because I have not sought the spotlight in my life, preferring instead the freedom I have had, so this was a big deal for me.

I felt what I was agreeing to, in part, was what I was supposed to be doing as the essence of myself. This was one of the reasons I had come to earth when I did and was something I needed to do to get my life right.

Jim, my life and business partner, was a bit chagrined and upset. I told him this was soul work I needed to do. I also had inherited some money from my mother's estate and therefore felt financially justified to make the decisions I was making. Today, Jim is most grateful that I did what I did. I, in turn, am most grateful that he did not initially give me his approval or support because it gave me an even greater opportunity to be as clear as I could be about what I should be doing at that time in my life and then to do it!

Inner divine guidance feels different than my ordinary thoughts. It comes from a different place too, one deep within my guts. It gives me a vaster picture than I usually have. Along with having depth, it is an expanded perspective that oftentimes includes the future. Its energy is like a sweep that comes up to my heart and then to my head, engulfing my whole body as it moves upward and outward.

In addition to inwardly hearing divine guidance, it also comes at times in the form of dreams, inner images, intuition, and direct knowing. What is direct knowing? It's when you just know. It is different than faith or belief. Direct knowing is stronger than intuition; there is an element of certainty about it.

The rule of thumb I use for my original perception and then subsequent translation of divine guidance is that it turns out to be positive for all those involved over time, if that is what they also choose.

This album of snapshots is being written within a continuous partnership with divine guidance in all its forms, for which I say, "Thank you, God!"

As I conclude this, Jim wants me to make absolutely sure to clearly state *we both believe everyone, no matter who they are or what they have done, has their own portion of God available that will lovingly give them divine guidance and assistance whenever requested.*

Living Life with No Regrets

Living my life with no regrets has been a marvelous pattern for me to use, both as an overall emphasis and as an evaluator.

When I was in my early twenties, one day I told myself that when I got to the end of my life, I wanted to be able to look back and have no regrets. It was one of the best decisions I ever made. Regarding important choices, it has helped give me the courage to do what I really feel right about doing and to not do what I would have later regretted.

This no-regret pattern has also been a continuous evaluative tool in minor ways. When I am shopping and see something I am not sure whether to buy, I always ask myself this question: "If I don't buy it, will I regret the decision later on?" If I answer "Yes," I buy it. If not, I don't. Now, since I am not a "shopper" and I only go looking when there is an occasion or need to do so, this process has worked for me. How it would work for someone else I don't have a clue. Here again, as with everything, I believe each of us has to find our own way.

My daughter, Kim, used a version of this no-regret pattern extensively during the two years her husband was involved with cancer. As she told it, she tried to live her life with David on a daily basis in ways to have no regrets, whatever the outcome of his illness. She focused each day as best she could on cherishing, treasuring, and celebrating what they had. Along with that, she sought divine guidance daily in morning journal-writing and prayer, out of which a channel of mental thought other than her own opened up for her. She felt this was the voice of her personal God.

When David passed on December 1, 1997, Kim was physically and emotionally drained. I think she recovered fairly rapidly because she wasn't involved with what so often goes along with grief—the regrets and "what ifs." Her deep grief was primarily centered on greatly missing David, and at the same time she was filled with gratitude for what they had shared in the time they did have together, both before and during his illness.

Which God?

Because there is such a huge belief in our culture that there is one God, it seems only natural that the idea each person has of God automatically is assumed to be what God is. Nevertheless, I think if each of us who uses a God concept described it, there could be large differences. I believe there is a transcendent realm of being, a divine source—God—and then, each of us who uses a God concept fills it with what we've been taught about God and with our own ideas about It.

A few years ago, I became more aware of this one day during a conversation with a man as he talked about God. I surprised myself by asking, "Which God?" He was taken aback and quickly said, "Well, God." Thoughts I had been only partially aware of were coming to the surface as I said, "Yes, God. But there are many ideas about who and what God is." After a moment of reflection, he nodded in agreement.

The God Jesus continuously talked about was a loving God, and over time I decided that would be my God, too. This is a major reason why I think about myself as a Christian. For many decades in my adult life, I had believed in God as an immense, powerful, loving, and transcendent source, but it wasn't until I also actively began thinking about a *personal* loving God that my life really took off.

At present I believe each of us is first of all spirit, a part of God as a whole, and as a spirit-person has our own portion of God that is vitally interested in our lives. This personal God is at the center of our beings, at our very core, and in order to activate Its presence to the degree where one is consciously aware of It, the person must purposely make the connections and then decipher Its messages.

This is a poem I wrote after the conversation with the man about which God.

MY PERSONAL GOD

My personal God is light,
        funny and friendly.
User-friendly.
My God is great company,
        with words of wisdom
        and well-chosen advice.

My God is fun.
It likes to have a good time.
Not at others' expense,
Just a good time.
My God likes to play.

My God nurtures and nourishes,
And likes to Be
        nurtured and nourished.

It's a blended relationship with us
    that flows both ways.
We both are enriched.
Oh yes.

"I" am one aspect of God as a whole.

My God's creativity
    is in lightness and darkness,
    force and gentleness;
    in the sun
    and in the rain;
    in the song of a bird,
    in the blossoming of a flower.
I can hear my God's voice
    in the sounds of the wind
        and
    in the sounds of moving waters.
I can see my God's message
    in a double rainbow.
My God's handiwork
    is everywhere
    and in everything.

My God is Divine Love.

God-Given Powers We All Use

To my way of thinking, the biggest God-given process each of us uses is when what we set forth in terms of our beliefs, ideas, intents, focuses, and thoughts of all kinds—along with emotions, inner pictures, and all the cultural tapes each of us carries within us—bring about the connections we make and our portion of the events of our lives. Each of us breathes energetic life into the patterns we use. *Therefore, we are both originators and experiencers at the same time.* I believe this process is a major way the universe works.

Another God-given process, which is connected with the first, is that where the focuses of the mind go, fueled by emotion, energy follows. Now, I think it is important to differentiate between the words a person uses and the operating patterns the person is really setting forth, oftentimes unconsciously and automatically. There are many situations when the two are not linked. Therefore, even though I listen to people's words, I also watch their actions and the results in their lives.

As I understand it, a God-given way of the universe is that we each operate on various wavelengths as the summary result of the thoughts and emotions we set forth. We oftentimes change wavelengths during the day, depending upon who we are with, where we are, and what we are originating.

This picture helps explain to me how I initially connect with some people and don't connect with others. For some time now, I have been intentionally eliminating long-held fears from my life, which I believe frees me from certain connections with others on that basis.

Overall, I think there is an ever-changing exchange and inter-play of energies between people as each of us lives out our daily moments and plays our part in relationships with one another.

Why Are We Here?

The best I can come up with as far as what I think we as spirit, as individualized portions of God, are doing here on earth is to provide ourselves and each other with experiences and contrasts. Then as we have our own experiences and see what others have done, along the way each of us as a spirit-person can choose freely which patterns we will use to form our own lives. Therefore, one can see oneself as having the opportunity to redesign one's life as one matures and grows.

I believe in general ways, before we are born, each of us as spirit has chosen our lives and parents for our own interests and purposes. When I took this as my starting point over twenty years ago, my life really changed.

There are some key ideas that have made the most sense to me up to this time. In the mind of God, any and all realities are probable and possible, but they are not filled out at that stage—they are lifeless models and patterns as probabilities. It is through our human-being originations and experiences in this system that we each give life and substance to some of these patterns. Hence, God knows Itself in action through our combined and cumulative lives. Therefore, everything has a divine origin.

Another part of this picture is each of us is here to remember ourselves basically as the spirit we are, to eventually peel off our accumulated cultural programming, and to bring our most filled-out divine selves forth in our everyday lives, whatever we conceive that to be. This then becomes an ongoing and evolving process.

When people talk about meaningful lives, I often fondly think of my mother. During the years I was exploring and talking about all of us having a purpose for our lives, Mother was absolutely clear her reason for being here was, as she said, "to have a good time."

Mother was certain she was here to have a good time, and within the context of her era and the life she lived, I think she did! She also provided joy and fun for those involved with her. She kept her childlike wonder throughout her life, which was blended with a lot of tough-minded practicality, forged from difficulties in earlier times.

Another picture came forth from our friend Irma, who recently visited us for a couple of days. Irma was born in Mexico and grew up there, coming to the United States to get her master's degree and Ph.D. She also lived in Spain in her early adulthood. She now teaches Spanish and Spanish literature at the university level. She sees herself as part of a new group of people who weave together understandings of many cultures, where it is not necessary to make one culture better than another. "Rather," she says, "in today's world it is important to understand the values of each one." She focuses on seeing each society as clearly as she can during her professional travels from the United States to Mexico and to Europe.

In one of our conversations, she told me she thinks each person is working on a puzzle in their lives. Everybody comes at their puzzle in a different way, from a different place—some from the middle, some from the side, and some from all over at the same time. As one part of the puzzle becomes clearer, one can add to that section, or focus on another part. When I asked her if she thought we all had the same puzzle, she said no. She thinks each of us has our own puzzle.

I liked the word picture she painted because oftentimes I have used the expression, "The pieces just fell into place, and I saw the bigger picture," or "The pieces just came together." I also liked her idea that each of us has our own puzzle to put together, where it is up to each person to figure out her or his own life.

Passing On

This is a poem I wrote on September 10, 1997, almost a year after my mother's passing on October 27, 1996. It has been vitally important for me to see life and leaving this life as a continuum.

CELEBRATING HER LIFE

Almost a year ago it was,
    in September 1996.
My mother was near the time
    to leave this life
    and move on to another one.
The doctor had diagnosed
    congestive heart failure.
She was eighty-four, stating emphatically,
    "I have lived a wonderful life!"
And I was on my way to visit with her,
    for the last time.

That Saturday at the book store
    while picking up a book
    as a gift to give a friend,
I was drawn like a magnet

to a book on the best-seller table.
I'm certain it was divine guidance.
With a day ahead of planned activities,
 I comfortably sat on a couch there—
 reading and reading and reading.
Finally an inward amused voice
 of common sense said,
"Why don't you just buy it?"
Of course. That's what I would do.

At home with much still to accomplish,
 I read and read and read,
Fascinated with the expansive story
 a woman told about her
 near-death experiences.
By that time I had highlighted sections,
 as I always do,
And, I knew I had to take the book to Mother.
So a fresh copy for her
 would have to be purchased
 before my flight Monday.

When giving the book to her I said,
"Honey, if this isn't your cup of tea,
 don't feel obliged to read it."
Her cup of tea it was,
Telling me it was very comforting
 for her to read
 these vivid accounts of the afterlife.

Mother said with a contented sigh,
"That's just how I always imagined
　　it would be."

We shared eight days together,
　　last September.
The weather was beautiful
　　there in Pennsylvania.
We looked at her photo albums
　　and tape-recorded her remembrances.
She, me, her granddaughter-my daughter.
There were four generations of us
　　all together—
Including her great granddaughter,
　　my granddaughter.

We celebrated Mother's life
　　as we toasted her at lunch.
We celebrated her life
　　as we drove in the country together.
We celebrated her life
　　with our hands holding one another's
And our eyes sending forth Love.
We celebrated her life.

On Sunday, October 27th, 1996
She had wine with her noonday meal
　　which she enjoyed greatly
　　at her assisted living facility.

71

In the early afternoon
    my son-in-law David came to visit.
And then, as she lay on the couch
    dressed in Sunday finery
    with him holding her hand,
Telling her we all loved her,
    she passed on ...
Just like that, peacefully.

At her request her body was cremated.
Her memorial service and buffet dinner
    were just as she had seen them
    weeks earlier in a dream—
Filled with people, music, good food,
    love, laughter, and tears.
With her favorite chocolate cake
    for dessert.

Yes, we still all celebrate her
    and her life
With gratitude, appreciation, and joy.

And we always will.

Spirit and Soul

After a lot of meditating, reflection, and rational thinking, I've come up with some definitions I want to present about spirit and soul.

For me, the spirit part of myself, when I think with the idea of time, is the portion that was part of God and somehow all the rest of us as spirit before my birth. The spirit portion of me is also at the center of me and my life here on earth and goes on after I leave this earth system.

The word "soul" for me means the intersection of myself as spirit and this reality system, both with the earth design itself and with the patterns we humans have constructed over time by using our God-given powers. My soul is the interaction of my individualized spirit with this reality system, where I am a spirit-person in this context.

An example of soul in operation as I am using it is what Jim is doing with his mother in the aftermath of his father's passing. The relationship and involvement Jim has with her right now seems to me to be soul work, where he knows himself and his mother basically as spirit, while at the same time he is honoring what they had and have in the physical realm as mother and son.

He and I both see this as a wonderful, precious period for him and for his mother, too.

A female friend of mine asked me whether I was jealous of the time and effort Jim puts into his relationship with his mother, and I responded, "Absolutely not! I think this is what he, in a spirit-person sense should be doing, where he now has the opportunity to translate all he has become. And of course the more he becomes, the better our relationship is!" Jim and I are also focusing on directly nourishing and treasuring each other and our lives together on a daily basis, as best we can with all we both have in motion.

At the soul level, I have come to realize I have the soul of an artist. I need to honor this. I thirst for the beauty and magnificence of the natural world and for what we humans bring forth in terms of beauty of all kinds, in multidimensional ways.

Within my worldview, there is a *big* difference between the level I am calling spirit and the level I am calling soul. At the spirit level, I always feel myself freshly engaged with God, whereas at the soul level there is a lot more going on. At the soul level, what I think is happening is somehow everything set forth by humans over the course of the history of the earth is all there, like in a big cauldron, and each of us on earth connects with portions of its contents according to our own programs and significances. I think the soul level is what Jung was addressing when he talked about archetypes and the collective unconscious.

Listening to and reading descriptions of other people's worldviews and experiences, in many instances it seems to me they mix the two levels or dimensions of spirit and soul together, when to my mind they really are distinct. I think it is very important to conceptualize and think about them both as valuable and, at the same time, different from one another.

Out of the many definitions the word "spirit" has in today's world is one that says there are nonembodied spirits who speak to and through sensitive humans. There are also said to be evil spirits. Others speak about their spirits as being a part of themselves but not basically them. In almost all the current-day definitions of "spirit," there is a mysterious quality beyond our physical and material world of the five senses.

As a contrast, what I am choosing to believe is that everything is filled with divinity and each of us is basically spirit, using our God-given powers of creativity in relationship with the design of the earth system itself and with others using their God-given powers.

In my life today, I am using a blend of understanding the cultural belief structures of the past and present as best I can, while continuously seeking fresh input from my portion of God. This is what I am calling my personal God, which I believe is vitally interested in me and my life.

Filling in Some Details

Problem-Causing Patterns

During the process of taking my life into my own hands over twenty years ago, I made some important-for-me discoveries. Since I was convinced my thoughts carried many of the keys to my life, on a daily basis I wrote out what came into my mind on large sheets of newsprint. What I began to see were belief constructions composed of many different designs. Then, as I took them apart and went deeper to their sources, I uncovered some of what I think are underlying, troublemaking cultural foundation patterns.

These are the large-scale, underlying patterns I discovered that I believe are part of our mutual cultural past and present in the Western world:

- dualism—opposites, oppositions, and polarities
- hierarchies—superiority/inferiority, ranking, elitism, and weighting
- automatic either/or thinking
- the belief there is only One Truth

In the following snapshots I will be describing how these patterns have played out in my life and how I think they play out in other people's lives, too.

Females and Males

The picture I see is that when we, as spirit, are born into this system as either a female or a male, each person is culturally trained for membership in one club or the other.

In addition to gender identification as a female or a male, one's identity is also culturally programmed with other pattern complexes, such as:

- what it means to be human, as defined by one's society
- her or his racial heritage
- the ethnic origin of his or her family
- the family's religious affiliations
- age beliefs
- the parents' social and economic class
- the parents' educational status or lack of

Then there are all the multiple pattern ingredients that fill out these complexes within the person's family and community belief structures. I think this large mixture of designs includes the connections one automatically makes with one's individual emphases at the soul level, where all past-present cultural patterns and models exist. Therefore, a person's current-day cultural designs are also invisibly and continuously fed at the soul level.

When I was around six or seven years old, I was told that girls were made of sugar and spice and all things nice while boys were made of rats and snails and puppy dog tails. Yes, this was said with an amused smile by women, and at the same time I knew it was more than just a saying or a joke. As I've looked back over my life, I think it was out of this female/male issue I made my first conscious decision to not buy into some of the cultural patterns. I can vividly remember thinking about my best friend, Dickie, who was certainly not rats and snails—and neither was my father. I also thought it sounded sickening to be sugar and spice and all things nice.

I didn't discuss this with anyone because I knew it would just get me into trouble. Instead, somehow I decided to think about myself and others first and foremost as people. Today, I wonder if back then I actually was connecting with my inner divine guidance, even though I had no such concepts to use at the time. (In those days God was far away "up there" and way too busy for my little problem.)

Jim and I have lived our lives smack-dab in the middle of the male/female dilemmas that have been swirling around all of us in one way or another since the 1960s. In 1977, off and on for about a year, we had a running battle over the issue of males' supposed inherent natural superiority over females. Jim was certain about the truth of his perspective, vividly pointing out the ways men could do things that were superior to what females could do.

Now most assuredly, my mother had done as good a job as other women of her generation in teaching their daughters about the male ego—to never directly tear it down and to build men up whenever possible. But somehow this way of thinking had never felt healthy to me. It seemed so disrespectful to both parties. And so I went to war with Jim over the issue of male superiority.

I heatedly and repeatedly pointed out that males were trained in our culture to be good at certain things while females were trained to be good at others. Jim's response was the male activities were more important than those of females. Therefore, male activities were more weighted, and males were superior to females. I *adamantly* refused to agree.

What happened over the course of the year is we both became a lot clearer and more aware of many of the facets of our gender training, including our subsequent thinking and actions.

As I look at the issue of male superiority/female inferiority from my viewpoint of today, I clearly see interwoven societal patterns of superiority and inferiority, rankings and weightings, opposites and oppositions, either/or thought processes, and the belief construction there is only One Truth.

This is a simple summary of some of the cultural agreements about male and female roles Jim and I discovered as adults, which we learned and used in some ways in our growing-up and adult years. (I was born in 1932 and Jim in 1933.) In my childhood, I was taught men and women in overall terms were opposites— that what one was the other wasn't.

Men were:
logical
hard

Women were:
emotional
soft

strong	weak
users of few words	talkative and gossipy
rational	intuitive
warriors	nurturers and peacekeepers
aggressive	passive
substantial	flighty
grouchy	sunny
practical	impractical
angry	pleasing and conciliatory
big decision makers	makers of all small decisions

A few years ago, I read a memoir written by a woman about three years younger than I am. The back cover talked about the time period she and I were adults in the 1950s when, it said, to be a woman meant, at best, to be a minor character in a drama played by men. I told Jim that sure struck a chord about my experience in those years! As women we were supposed to play parts where we primarily revolved around men and children—either as wives and mothers and/or as secretaries, nurses, and teachers.

In the later 1970s Jim finally agreed males were not *basically* superior to females, but he wanted females to become far more responsible than they had been culturally programmed to be in certain ways. I could see his point in terms of becoming more capable in areas that had been off my radar screen as a female in earlier years. For his part, Jim began to see the world differently, appreciating to a greater extent the skills and contributions of females. He, too, began to extend his capabilities into areas that had been off *his* radar screen when he trained in earlier years to be a male in our society. Nevertheless, it has continued to be an evolving process of modifying our attitudes and behavior. At points along the way, it becomes clear some of these earlier patterns have become activated again, needing present attention.

Another collision Jim and I experienced from our respective gender programming also occurred at times in the late 1970s and on into the early 1980s. He had been trained to be an independent, strong, decisive male. What this meant as far as I was concerned was that at times I felt he was very enclosed in what I called his own cocoon. In those instances, I believed in order to be heard by him about situations that were important to me, I had to bring a lot of energy to the event. In Jim's view it was like I brought the Army, Navy, and Marine Corps to the encounter, and in my view if he hadn't been so enclosed, I wouldn't have thought the extra energy was necessary to get his attention, understanding, and involvement in the first place.

In reality, I think Jim and my experiences of actions, reactions, counteractions, and on and on are all part of the same script males and females have been playing parts within for thousands of years in the Western world, and they all fit together. One lens through which one can see the above scenario between us years ago is if females over the ages had been more responsible, males wouldn't have been so enclosed. Males had been advised by other men, "Don't listen to women. They don't know what they're talking about." Another way to see the situation is if men had shared power equally, women would have had opportunities in which they could have learned how to be more responsible in the ways men were talking about.

The resolvement we agreed upon and implemented is one where Jim chose to be more open and available to what I was making significant and I chose to reduce my energies during our discussions, along with being more considerate of him in terms of when I brought issues forth. I also began to think more things through on my own ahead of time, before bringing them up for the two of us to consider and talk about. In our lives today, we are still playing/working with friendly-like discussions, which we don't always achieve, but the majority of times we do. Seeing ourselves and one another as basically spirit and spirit-people, with choices about the pattern constructions we use, has helped a lot!

From Jim's experiences and observations of others, he has thought most females have seen themselves much more as reactors to males than he thinks has been the reality. The step we took together was to think about ourselves as both being part of the same script, and when we stood back from the whole thing who could really say what was first cause? It seemed to us in certain ways it all happened at once, even though it played out sequentially over time.

And now I am usually able to mentally and emotionally hold both of our individual perspectives as being part of one larger reality, without having to defend my position, seeing value and validity for both of us in our respective viewpoints. I also see each of us as responsible for the worldviews we use and how they are translated.

While males have played the most visibly dominating parts in our Western world cultures for thousands of years now, I think it is equally clear that in the past three decades in the United States, the belief structures that have been supporting the male domination script have been crumbling.

I suspect there may be a second cultural revolution emerging, one that is still primarily under the surface. In today's world this may be coming from males who no longer are willing to live within their society-constructed enclosures. From reliable sources I read that overall, boys are faring less well in school than they did in the past. In addition, the rates of both depression and suicide for boys are on the rise. It seems many of them are questioning whether they want to spend their whole lives chained to jobs and male roles the way men in the past have been. Furthermore, some of them appear to be quite anxious in general about their futures.

My sense is that in the past, even though males were also put into cultural role boxes, there were a lot of perks for them, especially white males, in terms of societal self-esteem and a certain amount of independence and freedom. But in today's world there has been an accumulation of pressures from many directions that have been seriously challenging male dominance and authority, especially white male dominance. Some women and youth have been blaming males in general for most of the problems we face as humans in the present. And women who work outside the home or have at-home businesses have been expecting their mates to share more parenting and household activities.

I think there is a dualistic model for masculinity in America today. On the one hand males are supposed to be real men—to act tough, use anger and intimidation, be independent, and control situations in ways of the past; on the other hand they are now supposed to be in touch with their feelings, learn communication skills, and no longer play the parts of dominators, conquerors, and aggressors. It seems to me these conflicting messages can be very confusing. Along with all this, I hear that providing and protecting still continue to be large-scale focuses for many married men, especially those with children. "Provide and protect" were central themes for males in my parents' and my generation.

Females also are receiving many messages, some from the more distant past and some from the past thirty years or so, all of which are intermingling within each female, where different models and images emerge at different times.

I believe females are still being affected by patterns in use when I was growing up—to get large portions of their validation from males and male attention, especially the male they are with. In today's world, I hear men talk about how much continuous reassurance and admiration women want from them.

In my early adulthood, in major ways a woman's worth in her community was a direct result of the stature achieved by the man she married. Females were in competition—through their looks and actions—for men who would be good providers, status symbols, husbands, and fathers.

Out of our pasts, we females have many models for being in love. In one of them we become floaty and orbit around him, while he as a man in love is now a larger person with this addition to himself, and she is reduced in personhood terms. Another pattern I see we women use from the past is to equate love with being told we are needed by him, thereby feeling special and important. As I listen to women talk, I hear many of them unquestioningly think they have to have a man in their lives, fearing that to not have a relationship with a male, no matter what kind of a relationship it is, makes for an empty life.

More recently, females in the United States since the 1960s have been told we can be equals to men and can have it all—educations, careers, good jobs, and families. After using those designs, many women have discovered they can't do it all. In prior times when Jim and I were young adults, males focused almost all their energies into their jobs. So when women came into the work force in recent decades, there were established expectations based upon previous norms. Large numbers of women have been finding out they can't work a full-time job and then do what needs to be done at home, especially when there are children. In the past, when men devoted most of *their* time to their jobs, women spent their time taking care of the home and family.

Hence, today's females and males have together been forming new operating patterns that have been changing our society overall, and will continue to do so.

Amidst what is currently taking place in the United States are other currents in our tides of time. Since many females were in such a one-down and depowered position for so long, I see some women of today, along with stressing equality, trying to establish a beachhead in terms of superiority. They are pointing out they have been the nurturers and hence the good guys. They haven't been the ones to wage war.

Another way I see females establish their superiority and specialness is to combine an emphasis upon spirituality and love, as they say only a nurturing female can achieve. Even though nurturing is an area where most men have not had the training, practice, and cultural sanctions females have had, I believe men are perfectly capable of combining being spiritual, nurturing, and caring for others, even though it may not be just the way women do it.

During a recent conversation I told Jim that I think in one way or another each person has to grapple with the results of the use of the pattern of superiority and inferiority in America today. From my point of view it is part of almost everything and is usually combined with dualistic thought patterns and the idea there is only One Truth.

I believe there is no way males are going to let females be superior to them, even though male domination structures are crumbling. Males have been at the game of competition and winning or losing too long and are too skillful to let that happen. This includes the realm of spirituality and attempts to bring back the ancient times of the Goddess.

I think, as human beings, we are going to have to come up with new designs, different than those that have been used for thousands of years in the Western world. These designs can allow for the uniqueness of each person, while not using the stereotypes we learned about ourselves and "the other" when we trained for our gender club membership.

For decades I have been consciously making the choice to remove from my automatic thinking all patterns of superiority/inferiority, duality, either/or decision-making, and the belief there is only One Truth, while at the same time honoring the rights of others to choose what they do with their lives. As I understand how it all works, we humans have to use patterns. Nevertheless, as individuals we can choose *which ones* are to be the raw materials for our personal experiences, including how we think about ourselves and each other.

I believe it's a great idea to step back, lighten up, and see the humor and fun we all can have in writing new scripts for ourselves and the parts we play in our relationships.

Sexuality

When sexuality was culturally given to males in the past in the Western world as their supposed domain, within a dualistic way of thinking—where what one has the other doesn't have—at the outset it was a recipe for many problems. And we humans in both genders have been playing parts within the scripts that emerged from it for a long time now.

I have read that in England during the Victorian era, females who were about to get married were advised by their mothers to just lie back and think about something else, like the glory of England, when having sex with their husbands. Even in America in the 1950s, I've heard there was almost no mention of female sexuality in medical books—as if it just didn't exist in a natural way.

In contrast, males have been culturally programmed that sexual awareness should be on their mental front burners much or most of the time, in essence saying, "That's what it's like to be a normal male and a real man." Furthermore, there is a cultural consensus view that the more powerful the man, the stronger his sexual appetites and testosterone levels.

Then during the sexual revolution of the 1960s, some females declared they were just as sexual as males. However, I have questioned whether some females were attempting to match a male sexuality that had come out of an overall distortion in the first place.

I believe that sexuality is a natural human attribute. This picture became increasingly clear to me in my adulthood, so by the time I was in my early thirties, I made the conscious decision to not use *any* of what I considered to be hype around sex for my own life. I just lifted the whole cultural way of thinking about it out of my mental processes. Instead, I chose to identify with what I saw as my natural sexuality and lived my life discretely from that perspective. It is interesting to me that over the years I have met other women my age who had quietly made similar decisions about their own natural sexuality, moving beyond those times when there was a severe cultural evaluator about good girls and bad girls, and what was normal and what wasn't.

How all this translated out as far as Jim was concerned is that when he met me in 1970, he was vastly relieved to not have to be involved with any good girl/bad girl patterns from me. Therefore, from the beginning of our relationship we have had what we think of as an overall healthy and fulfilling sexual involvement with one another. Along with this, when he and I were amidst our gender clarifications over twenty years ago, he spent a considerable amount of time deciding what portions of his remaining cultural male sexual programming to keep and which ones to no longer use.

I do want to add that since anger and physical aggression were also given to males historically, as part of their supposed gender characteristics, when anger and physical aggression are combined with sexuality, the results have been disastrous for numbers of females, resulting in rape and abuse of all kinds. I also think this combination has been disastrous for the males who were and are the abusers.

A way to think about human sexuality is to use it as one avenue out of many through which divine love can flow back and forth with another person. Jim calls it a special kind of closeness. I agree with him.

Race, Prejudice, and Racism

Along with gender programming from birth, one's racial affiliation puts that person into a culturally constructed framework which includes all the beliefs about that race throughout history—both the good and the bad.

Here in the United States, one of the most long-standing and prevalent racial issues has been between whites and blacks—and our country's past of slavery. Another racial issue continuing from the past into the present is what happened between Europeans when they came to this land and the Native Americans, called Indians at the time.

Historically, the consensus of white Europeans was to view Africans as subhuman and those who were called Indians as savages. Both the Africans and the Indians were said to be from inferior cultures and were unlike the Europeans who saw themselves as civilized and superior. Patterns vividly in use in those days were superiority/inferiority, ranking, the weighting of the European reality, the belief there is only One Truth, and dualisms—all of which mixed together to distance them from other human beings. The Africans and Indians were "the other," different from those the white Europeans saw as being like themselves.

My large 1958 Webster's dictionary clearly shows duality and division into polarities—what one polarity is, the other polarity isn't—with its definitions of "white" and "black." The word "white" is associated with terms like happy, fortunate, honest, honorable, morally or spiritually pure, and free from evil intent. The word "black" is associated with terms like soiled, dirty, disgraceful, without hope as a black future, evil, wicked, and atrocious.

Yes, times have changed. Nevertheless, I think these definitions from 1958 continue to have a certain amount of power, oftentimes unconsciously as far as how we see ourselves and others. Individuals and groups continue to energize them both secretly and openly, along with unconsciously and consciously. These ways of thinking have been institutionalized, built into the fabric of our past and present.

I think no one likes to be looked down upon, and in a culture of ranking if one's position is not very high, one looks hard for opportunities to be superior. I suspect that the way females are portrayed as "hos" and "bitches" in gangsta rap songs is an example of superiority/inferiority in operation. In this case, black males who have been looked down upon are establishing superiority over females.

Moreover, I think these gangsta rap lyrics and their musical beat provide seductive messages young people often unquestioningly use to fashion their lives. Aggression is a central theme. It's like there is a big-time cool script that is being written with parts for both males and females to play. Some of these roles have even been given a type of heroic stature.

Obviously, over the centuries prejudice about other races and cultures emerged as the patterns of superiority/inferiority, rankings, dualities, and the belief there is only One Truth were set forth by our ancestors. As I see it, this includes the racism that continues into our current-day lives and will continue to play out in the future unless enough of us put a stop to it by consciously and effectively inserting different designs.

Ethnic, Religious, Tribal, and Language Affiliations

Recently, there have been many examples of the past being alive in the present in various regions around the globe. Ethnic, religious, tribal, and language differences intertwine in multiple ways, the result being people of one group sometimes become enemies of people of another group. These events have been occurring of late in the Balkans, in Ireland, the Middle East, and in Africa.

When people in the present feel honor-bound to revenge their tribal or ancestors' sufferings at the hands of others, then that's what they do—they pay the other group back. This can repeat itself for generations. And oftentimes leaders who are interested in amassing power for themselves use the opposing energies for their own purposes. Along with dualistic ways of thinking and beliefs in One Truth, superiority and inferiority patterns can also be a major contributor.

Going underneath some of the words used by people taking adversarial stands against others, it seems to me that fear is a large component. Oftentimes, individuals and groups of people are entrapped in cultural worldviews where they believe that if they don't kill, they will be killed. This then becomes their reality. The above picture also applies on a national scale.

Religious views can be especially powerful in people's lives. When Jim and I were amidst our cultural studies in the 1970s and '80s, we read many of the holy books of various world religions, seeing them as composites of belief patterns and also seeing them in historical terms as far as how these patterns played out on the world stage. From that perspective, we were usually able to answer our questions about why specific events took place when we understood the designs and worldviews used by the individuals and groups involved in each situation.

We discovered within many religions there were belief structures that their religion was special, relative to others. In some cases a religion has presented itself as being the true God-given one, while it is implied other religions are not the true one. These designs then set up potential difficulties. Many wars were fought in the past out of conflicting religious patterns, and some of those conflicts continue on in our present era.

According to the Old Testament, the Jews were special relative to others. It was said because of God's covenant with Abraham, they were God's chosen people. From the New Testament, the Christian belief structure has often been translated in ways where they were the special ones because of the belief that the only way one could be saved was through profession of Jesus Christ as one's savior. And then, the Muslims have built-in specialness for themselves among their belief patterns in the Koran.

Now from my perspective, if people assume there is only One Truth, it follows they may think they have to fight for their beliefs, when they actually have other choices. Another way of thinking is that by being a spirit-person, one can look at religious belief structures as ways to channel and experience one's divinity, but everyone doesn't have to do it the same way. He or she can treasure his or her own religious, ethnic, and tribal heritage while at the same time respecting others, in a horizontal manner. As individuals we can see ourselves and others first of all as spirit, seek inner divine guidance while we take our lives into our own hands, and from that position and perspective flow our lives forth.

Individually, we can choose to change the course of history by inserting different patterns into our current-day lives and into our souls. I believe it is in our daily lives and at the soul level enough of a critical mass of energies can come together to make the type of vast changes needed for a different future.

.

Good and Evil

Beginning early in my childhood, I puzzled and puzzled about evil: how to think about it and about people who commit acts that brutalize others and oftentimes themselves. Yes, I had certainly heard we humans were all tainted from birth because of the actions of Eve and Adam in the Garden of Eden, but somehow that way of thinking just didn't make sense to me. This was another area I didn't discuss with anyone and kept to myself. From my viewpoint of today, I think questions such as this set up internal energy charges, propelling me in some ways along my road of life. Later, when I was in college and had to choose a major, my choice was to major in history and minor in psychology. I think I was looking for understanding.

When stories started to emerge after World War II about Nazi Germany, I was incredulous that people could treat other humans the way the Nazis had treated Jews, Gypsies, and others. My horror also extended to what I learned about the treatment of Africans who had been brought to America and elsewhere as slaves.

It took me a long time, a lot of study, and a great deal of personal pain—but finally I got to the place where when I understood another person's worldview, I could clearly see why and how the person acted or acts as he or she does. On many occasions, in order to be true to one's own worldview and its pattern designs, a person believes he or she needs to wound and sometimes destroy others.

After I read Hitler's book *Mein Kampf,* in which he laid out major aspects of his belief structures—his thoughts and ideas about life—I was able to understand why and how he did what he did. Certainly, I didn't approve. No way! But I did understand that he believed he was doing a good thing by ridding the world of people he considered to be inferior and flawed. Connecting the dots, Hitler was strongly using a belief in the superiority of the Aryan Germans, along with using dualistic thinking, seeing other people in oppositional ways as inferior humans. There were additional elements of either/or thinking and One Truth perspectives.

Some people live as if the components of life are divided into two imaginary columns: one is Good and one is Bad, with the extremes in the Bad column being called Evil. Sometimes people see themselves as primarily bad or evil and act accordingly. Others see themselves as mostly good and act in the way they believe is good. But in a system that uses so much invisible and automatic duality, I think it is difficult to not somehow set forth both parts of the polarity.

At present, I see each person's psychic structure including many pattern constructions that are not always in harmony or communication with each other. He or she can energize one grouping at times and at other times a different group, without remembering the earlier one. Frequently, the person doing so is only aware of and identifying with just one part of what he or she is setting forth. Because I believe it is wise to establish conscious connections and a conversation between the various elements in one's psychic contents, in "Rage, Betrayal, and Understandings" I will be describing a process I effectively used decades ago to do so.

Personally, I think the categories of "good and bad" and "right and wrong" can provide an *individual* moral compass if they are used to link up actions with results, instead of just calling something good or bad. It seems to me that when a person expands what is right and good for him or her out as a moral imperative for others to use, one can get into judgmentalness and righteousness. To my mind, there is a vast difference between seeing situations clearly in terms of their various aspects and making decisions for doing what is personally right, as contrasted with judging others as right or wrong.

In raising children, the emphasis can be upon *kindly* showing them how pattern designs work, along with what results their actions bring about in their own lives and the lives of others. In my opinion, our world needs large doses of kindness and comprehensive understanding!

My heart goes out to children and adults who have somehow drawn the conclusion they themselves are bad. This usually happens because they have been told that repeatedly in their childhood. Once this perspective about themselves becomes an embedded operating pattern, their thoughts and actions flow out from there. I would love to see people of any age who are living out of this assumed bad position choose differently: to be spirit-people in partnership with inner divine guidance, restructuring themselves and not having to be what others have said or say they are. This can be done by anyone, from any position. Yes, it's a big challenge, and it also can be seen as a big opportunity.

I do believe those who abuse others always have different options, even though it may not seem so from the worldviews they are enclosed within. Here again, they too can restructure themselves, proving their sincerity over time with consistent actions.

Even though I've talked about cocreativity in terms of events, I think it's a very complex issue that goes into who one believes oneself to be, how much self-awareness the person has, what mental and emotional patterns she or he uses, and other dynamics I don't know about.

The Ego

There is talk about getting rid of the ego in some spiritual belief structures. Nevertheless, I think it is needed. As I define the ego, it includes how a person thinks about her or himself in her or his society, and it is the portion of each human being that interfaces with her or his family and community. It has come about from a person's cultural programming and from the interpretation of what he or she has experienced in life. *Here again, as with our mental processes, what is important is the content of our egos. I believe that with focused intent, anyone can change its content.*

Expanding out, small groups and larger groups such as nations can have egos that they feel beholden to protect and defend, just as individuals do. Nationalism can have many hierarchical and dualistic components.

The females of my generation were advised never to tear down the male ego and whenever possible to build up the man's image of himself. What became clear to me over time was how basically fragile egos are to need that type of coddling. Moreover, males who are flattered in those ways don't have the opportunity to become wholer and stronger in other ways. To be sure, we females also have our ego vulnerabilities.

One of the results that came out of studying the contents of my thoughts decades ago was more clarity about what I thought of myself, the contents of my ego. I discovered a lot of polarities. At one point I said, "What a mess!" I also discovered many old designs that were no longer in my best interest, so I removed those I no longer wanted to carry around with me and hence set forth as part of my contributions to life events. Over the years, I have thoughtfully reconstructed my ego. I'm not aiming for perfection, and I am easy on myself. My goal at first was to have a healthy ego, and then I added that it be aligned and harmonized as best I could with myself as spirit and with others as spirit.

My ego doesn't build itself up at another's expense. It is open and not fragile. However, I don't stay directly connected to people who use patterns of abuse with me—physical, mental, emotional, psychological, or philosophic. My ego sees itself, along with my mind and physical body, as the representation of major aspects of me as spirit in this reality system—and it loves its part!

As far as Jim's ego is concerned, I tell him when I think he looks good or has done something well. Then, when I have something to say that may be difficult for him to hear, I try to choose the time and my words with care. I and my ego like to be recognized when my physical appearance is attractive and in multiple other ways, too. Nevertheless, I do what I do in terms of getting my life right and usually am able to let go of what I set forth without strings attached.

I truly believe there is room for us all to express and experience ourselves uniquely and individually as spirit and spirit-people in this system—in our families and communities, nationally and globally—without using opposition, ranking of oneself relative to others, superiority/inferiority, and a belief there is only One Truth.

Rage, Betrayal, and Understandings

This is the story of how I began to detach myself as the essence of myself from my cultural patterning, even though I didn't consciously know that was what I was doing at the time. What I did know was I somehow had to get myself out of a huge crisis situation.

It was 1978. Jim and I had been living in the western foothills of the Sierra Nevada mountains in northern California since the late summer of 1975. We had built a modest home there on three acres amidst a hundred-acre woods. I had quit my teaching job, and Jim had continued with some of his financial planning clients in southern California, partly because he still was obligated to pay child support.

We had exchanged money-making and money-spending for time. Some of the time we freed up was used to do a lot of exploring. In 1976, we had taken a six-state month-long trip of backpacking and camping in various wilderness areas. We also had hiked and investigated the areas around where we lived—the rivers, the flow of water, soil erosion, the economy, ecosystems, and the interconnectedness of life. Then in 1977, off and on for about a year, Jim and I battled about the so-called natural superiority of males relative to females.

The crisis in 1978 came from my fully realizing my father was nearing the end of his life, and I was so angry at him that I didn't want to see him. But I also loved him greatly and couldn't let him leave the earth feeling the way I did about him. I knew I had to shift something.

My starting point was that I was furious with my father! As I got into the contents of my anger, I discovered that what I felt was betrayal by him. How could he have taken the love we had and used it as he had done to manipulate and hurt me? How could he!

It was during the long, agonizing, and liberating process I then went through, as I understood the context of his times, his life experiences, and what he had made out of those experiences, I knew why he had done what he did. *He had been a prisoner of his own worldview, and I had been one of his primary dancing partners as his only child. As this understanding emerged, I also made the conscious decision to see myself as the essence of myself, having chosen my parents for my own reasons before my birth. That design really changed and reorganized things! Over time, I went from being a victim to the initial stages of being an empowered spirit-person.*

The process was extensive. I had a lot to do! Jim, who has played golf throughout his life, says you don't play the eighteenth hole until you play the other seventeen. I am adding that one also has to have the right golf clubs, skills, intent, and attitude. As I see it today, the reason I was able to stick with what I was doing was because I experienced it as a psychological life-and-death matter. I knew I couldn't live with myself if I didn't come to some type of resolution over this issue. And when the process was complete, I felt relief and elation.

Afterward, I viewed the results as being those of which I was the proudest in terms of accomplishment up to that time.

Before I revisit the past any further, I want to talk about the question a friend of mine has asked me on occasion: Why, if we choose our parents as spirit, do some people give themselves such awful lives? Said with compassion, my answer is that it's really each person's choice whether to think that way and to explore for him or herself.

At first when I decided I, as the essence of myself, had chosen my parents, I did so because at some level it felt right and made sense to me. Then I set out to discover why. For me, it had to do with experiences I wanted to have and lessons I wanted to learn for comprehensive, expansive understandings. And for my evolvement in spirit-person terms.

I now believe my parents were the perfect people for me. I think, as spirit, when I looked at probable futures on the earth before my birth, I saw a vivid one that attracted me. It was one where new songs and new stories could be set forth, and I-as-spirit wanted to play a role and have experiences within it. Among the various probabilities, I wanted to be a player in bringing forth different patterns for females and males than had been available, and I wanted to have *those* experiences. What opportunities there were!

One of the first things I did back in 1978 was to decide to take my life into my own hands. I felt I had a lot of raw materials with which to work. Along with our explorations of the natural world, Jim and I had been exploring what was taking place culturally. Some of our activities had included experiencing nearby Yogic ashrams, setting up our own meditation practices, and participating once in a five-day workshop for integrating mind, body, and spirit at Esalen, the growth center at Big Sur, California. Additionally, we had been involved in body movement and dance activities with others in our area. Moreover, I had been using an intuitive process of turning myself loose in bookstores, connecting with an eclectic mix of books from which I read and culled out ideas for experiments and activities that seemed potentially valuable.

As I described in "Problem-Causing Patterns" and "The Ego," by the time of my 1978 crisis I was convinced my thoughts carried many of the keys to my life. On a daily basis, I sat down and wrote out on big sheets of newsprint what came to my mind. Then I would go deeper into their sources, wherein I discovered some of the underlying patterns that were troublemakers for me and appeared to be problems for other cultural members, too. I kept notes of the patterns I removed and those I replaced them with, linking up changes to my life experiences in the future.

I learned that each part of a design was significant and had effects upon the other parts. Some of my favorite patterns were flawed in those ways. I also learned there was no danger in removing cultural designs as personal operating materials for my life—they stayed around and were available for conversations. I came to the conclusion that humans have to use patterns. The question is, which ones are they personally fueling?

Over time, I began to conduct daily workshops for myself, beginning around 9:00 a.m. and ending around 11:00 a.m. It seemed like a good idea to have a structure such as this and to then go about the rest of my life. Otherwise, I think a person can become overly focused in one area.

I interpreted my dreams as messages from deeper layers of myself. I oftentimes used the technique of acting out each symbol in the dream and then dialoguing between the parts as I moved to different positions in the room, with one player being a Wise One who offered valuable comments and suggestions. I had many conversations with my father in this way, playing his part as best I could, moving back and forth between him and me in the room. Sometimes I would go back in time to earlier ages in my life, playing out scenes differently than they had occurred, which always somehow gave me a feeling of increased potency in the present.

The technique of having conversations was also useful in terms of connecting various pattern components of my psychic structure, giving voice to each of them, where they could dialogue among themselves. I could then become *consciously aware* of what had been and was internally taking place. There was an additional goal of forming an integrating and harmonious internal consensus, where the voice from the Wise One made valuable suggestions for the rest to consider.

When I finished for the day, I would make a few notes as possibilities for the next day, but it wasn't until I got to the next morning that I would decide upon the initial contents for my activities, which then became a developing process.

By the time I started the explorations of my thoughts and the daily workshops, I had already tried beating pillows and yelling at my dad to discharge my anger. But this only relieved my pressures temporarily, leaving me tired and basically unsatisfied.

It also became distressing for Jim, even though I was using the downstairs bedroom. He firmly requested I do something else. His input added to my own motivation to be more effective.

From my perspective of today, one of the most liberating things I did to disengage myself to some degree from my own patterns was to occasionally put on a whole new set of designs with which to interface with the world. Some days I would write down a set of patterns I was going to use, temporarily set my own aside, and go off for a walk in the woods to see the world through different filters. Sometimes I would use what I knew about my father's core worldview. At other times, I would use what I had heard or read another person say about themselves that seemed to be part of their core beliefs. Then when I came back I would become "me," review the patterns I had used, and write about my experiences.

Also, at times I would go for a walk in the woods and to the nearby meadow with a pond, while purposely pulling the essence of myself out and behind my body, identifying with myself as the essence of me. When I pulled my consciousness out of my body, I did so by sending it a message of trust—believing it knew what it was doing and didn't need me for that period of time.

How did I come up with these ideas? Some came from things I read, some came from what happened during my workshops, others occurred to me while gardening, baking bread, walking in the woods, or in the company of other people. I used to say I was turning around in my psyche in a 360-degree manner. Today as I see it, I was both open and seeking divine guidance, which I think I received on a continuous basis. In those years, I did not have a personal God such as I have now. What I had then was a fundamental faith in an immense, loving God, and I immersed myself within It.

Over time, my rage, anger, and sense of betrayal diminished. I understood why my dad had done what he had done. My understandings didn't make it right, but when I saw what a prisoner he had been, those understandings and compassion replaced what I had been feeling before. I think I allowed the Love I felt for both of us to begin to move and flow more fully through the new channels of penetrating understanding.

From my viewpoint of today, all those activities worked together, including daily meditation. The enormously healing aspects of my growing relationship with the natural world and the time I spent within it were a big factor, too.

Finally when I had made enough changes, I called my parents and said I would like to come to southern California for a five-day visit. I remember how brave I felt at the time—I was going to *stay* with them for five days! Before I left home, I prepared a small index card upon which I wrote a few key thoughts such as "My father is dying. I will not get in a fight with him." "I will show my love to my father." "I will not let my father emotionally or psychologically abuse me." "I will be firm, fair, and centered." I kept the card in my purse during my visit, and when I felt myself getting off-base, I would go into the bathroom, take some deep breaths, and read over what I had written until I was cohesive again.

During 1978, and through September 1979 when my father passed on, I think I visited my parents five times for periods of around five days. On occasions it was quite difficult, and at the same time, it was enormously rewarding. I was able to share in their lives as I listened to Dad talk about the past and his life experiences. I heard his bewilderment about the changing world and the changes I was making. I think his worldview had become extensively fixed and rigid. In response to many of the concepts I was using, he would shake his head and say, "I just don't understand."

For years prior to the time of my visits to them, I had been aware that one is still being controlled by a cultural agreement when one is rebelling against it, but I hadn't really developed enough of a coordinated group of replacements for the patterns I had learned in earlier years. By the time I was with my parents in the later 1970s, I had been forming my own worldview a piece at a time, with harmonizing elements in place that felt good to me. Therefore, I wasn't just responding or reacting to theirs. Even though Dad said he didn't understand, I think both of their thoughts about how it all works were affected by mine in expanding ways.

My father had grown up in a Midwestern farming community where his maternal grandparents had three farms. He was born in 1911, the second child, with an older sister. His father died when he was very young. Dad felt his mother had never given him the love or care he should have received. Nevertheless, he had some love from his grandparents and had been told by them he would have the necessary money for a college education—and then some. It was from that perspective he proposed to the young woman who would become my mother—they both could go to college. They were married in July 1930. Mother had just turned eighteen, and Dad was almost nineteen.

By that time, his grandfather had already passed on. According to my father, when his grandmother did the same, his mother and her sisters plotted so he didn't get any money.

I was born in October 1932. Mother had been seriously ill during her pregnancy, weighing eighty-some pounds at my birth. Just before I arrived in the world, the doctor asked my father which one of us he wanted him to save in case it came to that. Dad often dramatically described how he told the doctor, if either one of us died, he would kill him. I think if I had been the doctor, I would have believed him. My father was a small-statured man who had learned how to use the force of his anger to do what he thought should be done. Over the years, I learned he was using his version of standard operating procedures for men in those days.

Dad was working at the time of my birth. But as the story goes, when he came home every night, he happily took over my care from my weakened mother. I think he adored me, but as I understand the designs males used in those times, I think he also saw me as his possession and in certain ways *there for him.*

When I was an adult, Mother told me that during their courtship, she only saw the charming, intelligent, good-looking, "decent young man" qualities of her future husband, but then after they were married, the darker side of him came out. She termed it his "Dr. Jekyll and Mr. Hyde" personality. Yes, she said, after a while she had seriously questioned her choice of a husband, but she had been a child who had been scarred with the shame she felt because her parents had divorced. Also, she often-times told me there is something wrong with everyone, so I think she decided the positive outweighed the negative. Moreover, I believe there was a great deal of divine love between them.

I was an only child.

Dad was out of work most of the time when I was three (1935–36). This was during the Depression. Mother worked at the local department store, where the husband of one of her friends was the manager. Dad was home with me most of the time that year, and I still can remember the delight we shared. I think he was a natural-born teacher. I had a blackboard upon which he showed me letters and numbers. He was patient and warm. I rapidly learned to read books. We cooked and baked together, colored together, and just had a good time. We were pals.

As I grew older, I think my father's life crowded in on him more. Over the years, he told himself on a daily basis how badly he had been treated by his mother and her sisters—and how angry he was. I think he fed himself daily doses of psychological and emotional poison, which then affected him physically over time. I also think he believed he had suffered so much that it somehow was his due that someone—like me—make him happy. He was owed.

My feelings of betrayal, hurt, and anger came from my thinking he took the deep and connective love we had and used it to emotionally abuse me, try to manipulate me, and to give himself a feeling of power. When I was in my teens, he seemed to enjoy dumping his everyday life frustrations on me at the dinner table, oftentimes reducing me to tears with a stomach in chaos.

Sometime during adolescence, a way of thinking came about for me where I saw myself as having a small steel ball at my core.

No matter what went on, it was impenetrable. Verbal abuse could not invade it in any way, so I had given myself some protection.

Over the years, I think my mother unconsciously developed some protection for herself in the form of rheumatoid arthritis. She would have an arthritic attack if she became emotionally upset. It became a way for her to keep my father somewhat in check. She noted in her later years how much healthier she was after his passing.

When I was eight months pregnant in 1957, Dad telephoned one day to tell me he was calling to purposely upset me, "so your mother will pull herself together." She had just received news that *her* father had died, and she was taking it very hard. In my opinion, all of her ambivalence about him had come to the surface. Mother had developed a strategy throughout her life, based upon a belief there was no use crying over spilled milk, of "putting things out of her mind."

My father ranted and raved about how I somehow should have known all this was going on and been a better daughter. After that phone call, I said to myself with every fiber in my being, "I am going to break this cycle of sickness I've been trapped within!! I'm getting out!" Today, I'm sure I set up a lot of energy which has been ever-present over the years with that determined decision I made in 1957.

One of the things I discovered is that it was not enough to break a cycle of sickness—I needed to replace it with health.

I think a core pattern my father used was that the world is a hostile place, out of which, at least in part, he lived his life and made connections. He also believed there were kind and good people, but somehow he'd been unlucky to have been with some "bad apples" in his earlier years. Both my parents believed in a remote God "up there."

As I grew up, I had a mixture of beliefs. I knew things weren't as extreme as my father painted them, but I didn't have a clear picture of how to think about the world. People certainly didn't talk about belief structures and worldviews in those days!

Later, when my marriage was dissolving in the 1960s, I went into therapy to have a place to hopefully make more sense out of my life. Some of the patterns being used at the time within the humanistic psychology community seemed better than the ones I had been using. I tried many of them out and then experienced the results. This is when I learned the design that mental processes were suspect and emotions were what one should emphasize and be aware of. I'm truly grateful to the therapist, who in our fifty-minute weekly session focused me on the here-and-now, where I became very clear about my emotions and their changing tapestry. Over time, I used that important *self-awareness* skill with my mental processes too, eventually seeing the interconnections between the two.

In this snapshot I've focused extensively on the circumstances that provided the fuel for me to take my life into my own hands in the late 1970s. Now, it's time to fill in the overall picture more fully. Along with the times of mental and emotional abuse, I also lived a really good life. I think there is a cultural tendency to greatly magnify the negative—I know I did!

With persistence, Dad had refused to see girls as intellectually inferior to males. Since he was forever regretful about not having gone to college, it was extremely important to him that I go. I happen to think his emphasis upon education—my education—was a *very* valuable motivation in my life. Mother told me in my teens that she didn't believe in females getting more formal education because it limited their chances to get a good husband.

Mother was a small, slender, petite, attractive, charming, and feisty woman. She also was practical and what at the time was called "strong minded." To this day I can still hear her say, "I just made up my mind," which meant there was a lot of determination behind what she intended or didn't intend. She had absorbed hundreds of cultural patterns, both consciously and unconsciously, most of which she passed on to me. When I began to explore my thoughts in the later 1970s, I found dozens of inner tapes I had incorporated from her training.

In the years when I was playing around with the idea of reincarnation, I could see Mother having lived a probable life in a French court. She had a passion for clothes and shoes, light-hearted music, gaiety, beautiful works of art, chocolate, champagne and other wine, and being entertained. She also loved being amidst the beauty of the natural world—flowers, the oceans, deserts, and mountains. I was so pleased for her when, after my father passed on, one spring she toured Europe, with an emphasis upon beautiful flower gardens. Of course, she adored Paris. She also enjoyed her experiences during a trip to the Hawaiian Islands and a cruise in the Caribbean.

Many of my dad's emphases became focal points of my life. Without them, I wouldn't be who I am. Today, I see him as basically spirit. I am *deeply* grateful for our relationship and the part he played in my life.

My father's passing, early one Saturday afternoon in September 1979, was without his usual drama. When my mother came out of the shower, he was slumped in the hallway with a beautifully peaceful look on his face. That morning, he had received a card I had sent him expressing my Love again. I like to think I, too, played my part well as spirit and a spirit-person.

More Pictures

Primal Processes

During the months of May and June 1999, I stopped directly focusing on this book of word pictures I was compiling. I had been receiving some strong divine advice that it was the time to turn my attention to other areas. Even so, new snapshots emerged. Again, I wrote them down as raw materials on yellow sheets of paper to decide what to do with later.

In April, on repeated occasions, I had been given an inward, unexpected go-ahead to take a once-a-week, eight-week watercolor painting class. I was thoroughly delighted. Furthermore, there were many books I had piled up to explore *sometime*. I could see this was the time to read at least some of them. Also, I was experiencing a few less than fully healthy physical conditions. It seemed to me they had come out of some imbalances in my life.

Health in all its dimensions became a main centrality during my time-out. I believe by selecting an emphasis, in this case health, it becomes an inner field force for communications and energy connections. One then draws to oneself what one is focusing upon, and one's overall activities can have a coordinated wholeness about them. I could see myself further filling out the process I started in 1957 when I vowed to break the cycle of sickness I felt I was entrapped within, which later became an emphasis upon being healthy in all ways. I also continued to remove any debilitating cultural beliefs I still energized about aging, opening the system up to see what would happen in terms of health and vitality.

I knew this pause period would be one where at times I would just show up, discovering myself and the next step to take. As I had done in the later 1970s, I held some morning workshops, but this time it wasn't every day. One of my focuses was a continuation of previous explorations I had begun a few years ago about primal or primary processes, because I have had a generalized understanding that there are basic processes we humans all use. On various occasions during the past few years, I have played around experientially with what they might be. Three of them I have delved into are sound, movement, and individual expressions of multiple kinds. Moreover, I believe our human bodies are focal points for experiences and are actually energy transmitters in this system, where our spirit creativity comes through physical forms.

In addition to personal processes, there were two big events during my time-out that captured my attention and the attention of many other people, too. One was the continuing tragedy in Europe, in the Balkan region of Kosovo. The other was the tragedy in the United States in Littleton, Colorado, where two white male teenagers killed twelve fellow students and a teacher at their high school, before killing themselves.

To my mind, the situation in the Balkans was a direct example of what I talked about in "Ethnic, Religious, Language, and Tribal Affiliations," where groups of people war with one another using patterns from the past that are active in the present.

One of the messages I translated from what took place in Littleton is that everyone wants to be valued, respected, and divinely loved. As I understand the story, the two Littleton teenagers felt they had been humiliated and wrongly treated—pushed out by insiders into the outsider category. I'm certainly not saying what they did was O.K. No way! What I am saying is that within my worldview I'm now seeing horizontal valuing and respect for others as a primal process, going to the roots of life.

My watercolor class was marvelous. I use a pattern that when the student is ready, the teacher appears. Is it any wonder my teacher was perfect for me at this time? All my life I have had some artistic talent in terms of drawing and painting, but there were very few occasions where I felt it was appropriate for me to explore those realms and develop my skills. So, I was starting from scratch in terms of kinds of paper, quality and makers of paint, and other such matters.

One of the things I knew I would be doing when I took the class was to more directly activate my right brain, the portion that is nonverbal, musical, artistic, and thinks in whole pictures. Even though I certainly do use large portions of it, at the same time the central focuses I have been making for a number of years have been into spirit-based depth and left-brain activities such as language. I felt it was time to be more balanced. My emphasis in painting also synergized with the physical movements and sound I was exploring in my current personal workshops, most of which were without verbal language.

Our teacher had us start out with large sheets of paper, first wetting them with a brush and then painting skies. The purpose was to open each of us up. In a portion of a poem I wrote titled "Watercolor Reflections," I said:

Watercolor play is
    increasing my skills
    with fluidness and flexibility.
I'm continuously aware of
    cocreativity—
    me, water, color,
    paper,
    images and forms.
Discoveries keep emerging of
How much I want
    subtle and beautiful shapes,
    luminosity and flow in my life.
I also love the joy I experience
    when unexpected surprises happen.

As I layered color, I saw life that way, too, where some layers and areas are darker and denser than others that are lighter. Watercolor is also like life because one can change what one is doing and go in a different direction.

An art class event was very funny later on but wasn't so funny when it happened. At the end of a session, our teacher told us to bring in something for the next class to paint in a grid, repeating the image several times. She showed us a few examples of what she meant. I was less than enthused but tried to make the best of it. I brought in a butterfly pin I am very fond of and a butterfly book by a French artist for inspiration. I also brought a smaller piece of paper, thinking I wouldn't have to do so many of them. Nevertheless, the teacher wanted me to use the regular-size paper to which I quietly and unhappily agreed. About as creative as I got during most of the exercise was to draw butterflies in different positions in the individual sections and in one case to draw two butterflies.

Then something happened. While I was working on the background of the fourth section, where I already had painted the two butterflies, all of a sudden I started playing with the very lovely turquoise paint I was using. I found myself dabbing away in a rhythmic movement as I realized what fun I was having.

The next morning at home I told myself, "I need to play today. I need to have a playday!" I immediately cut out the rectangle of the two butterflies with its turquoise background, taped it temporarily from the back onto another sheet of larger paper, and painted a multicolored, harmonious, formless background around it, expanding out from the turquoise I had felt joy with the previous afternoon.

The week before, I had been at the University of Michigan's Museum of Art, where I had seen Helen Frankenthaler's *Sunset Corner*, a very large acrylic on canvas painting done in 1969. It was hung in the "Twentieth Century Art" area in the museum. I read in the painting's description about color being freed from the crafted bounds of figurative shapes and surface textures. The morning I released the two primitive butterfly figures from the confines of the grid and allowed myself to play with color, when I was finished, I could see forms emerging from color and color unleashed from forms.

Later, when I reflected about this event and process, I knew some dynamic shifts had taken place within me that would affect my whole life. I had not accepted pain and boredom. Obviously, at some level I saw my lack of interest as a signal to change direction. Then, one evening not long afterward, while floating in the bathtub, I realized with a jolt that it is no longer a matter of me opening the whole thing up. Somehow I am much more open now. What a thrilling discovery! There are times I feel tingly with delight.

The dreams I experienced during this period seemed to be fuller and more comprehensive, of a wholecloth. When I finished the class and looked at the overall results of what I had painted, I discovered in almost every case I had brought in a type of fourth dimension, a light and movement from the spirit level. Even though I had been vaguely aware of what I was doing at the time, it wasn't until I stood back that I had a clearer view of what had been coming forth.

Recently, a female author I heard at a book reading talked about her perspective where we all need to be more human, instead of trying to get away from life. Her words struck me so strongly it was as if a Chinese gong went off inside, reverberating ever since. I don't know exactly what this means, but I know I like vitality, vividness, and dramas of *certain* kinds. And I also love being human.

Jim's Odyssey

Near the end of May 1999, during the first month of my two month time-out, while I was emphasizing health and primal processes, Jim became dramatically ill. His symptoms were large amounts of stomach pain, along with breaking out in weltlike hives all over his body. Now Jim is a good-sized man, six feet tall and around two hundred pounds—so he was quite a sight! Later he termed it a spiritual crisis, where conflicts he had never been able to resolve came full-blown to the forefront.

At the time, one of the books I was reading, part of the stack I had been accumulating, graphically portrayed the rampant existence of male depression in our culture, both the obvious and the not-so-obvious. Certainly, Jim and I honor one another in terms where each of our lives is our own, and at the same time we offer ideas we think may be of value. Since I was quite concerned, I read portions of a chapter aloud to him, where the male author who is a family therapist described some current-day situations in men's lives and in their relationships with their families.

After listening to that part of the book, I was surprised when Jim said he wanted to read the whole thing himself when I was done. Some of my surprise came from my past experiences with him where he doesn't buy into most psychological theories, and the rest because he was enormously busy with what he had on the plate of his life. I was almost finished with it. When I gave it to him, he set aside what he had been concentrating on to read it nearly straight through. Afterward he said, "This is an amazing description of the patterns for use by males in our culture—and the results of their use."

Immediately, he began putting together a series of writings for the purpose of opening up perspectives about himself and his life. He titled them, "Healing and Integrating My Whole Encultured Self—Memorial Weekend 1999." The following are excerpts from what he wrote.

He began by saying, "As I look within myself what I find is myself as spirit, and an enculturation process that has taken place for many generations which has many facets. As spirit I am myself as loving, caring, unformed and forming creativity, being in an infinitely beautiful, supportive, infinitely loving environment which has no harshness as part of its emotional content, and is infinitely enjoyable and fun. This is the heart and soul of my being, and remains my home base, my center, which also is available to permeate all aspects of my being. I am that in all ways. And as I look inside at my enculturation I see patterns and designs of function and emotion I have used to route, direct, and color myself as spirit."

In his first writing, of what would turn out to be a series of four, Jim then went into his past with the understandings he has acquired over the years. He saw how his father had passed onto him, his son, the designs his father had learned. In his writing he sadly concluded, "That was very difficult for me because what I wanted was a loving closeness rather than an authoritarian model ... even so, as I review my life I see I never completely subdued myself as spirit."

Jim saw the brutality that took place to enculture him as a male, which oftentimes was done with loving intent. He saw himself as fighting and competing his way through elementary school while still being spirit. His perspective about himself was even though there was a lot of trauma, he was an adventurous spirit who wanted to try new things, go into new territory.

He saw his relationship with his first wife as being filled with highly conflicting energies of all kinds, with conflict and tension being its centerpoint. He sadly reflected that this was the environment into which their children were born.

Major emotions he identified over the years within his childhood home and in his first marriage were love, anger, guilt, and sorrow.

As he wrote, he became vividly aware he now needed to harmonize all aspects of himself, to become reunited as spirit from a spirit perspective with all the love, understanding, and caring available from that perspective. He continued to go deeply within, talking about the love he feels for us all and for himself.

Jim's second writing during the Memorial Day weekend of 1999 started out by saying, "As I look back over my years as Jim, there was a major delineation and change when I met Jacquie in 1970. Prior to that time I had completely played out my cultural life. I had tried all the cultural designs and ways of being I cared to try, had played out my male-centered success designs to the point where I hated the content of the relationships I was then forced to deal with, and as I looked to the future in that environment was sickened by what I saw if I continued. Then as far as male-female relationships are concerned, I had tried many varied connections through the years to the point where they were all too limiting and uninteresting to me.

"It seemed to me so many people were living lives with varying degrees of desperation and unhappiness, within culturally patterned confines which were strangling and deadening them. I was one of those people who felt so confined as I played out my culturally patterned string, I got to the point where I really didn't care whether I lived or died. If I had stayed in that way of life, I most likely would have left this world with my car flattened against a bridge abutment on some expressway, freeing myself from the deadness of continuing within the narrow confines of this culturally defined world. If I were to continue living I had to free my spirit, or else I would leave this world and free myself as spirit that way. This is when I met Jacquie.

"The weekend we met (on a Saturday afternoon beside the swimming pool at the Spa Hotel in Palm Springs, California when Jim was at a business conference and I was there with two female friends), and the summer we intermittently spent together, were the beginning of my freeing my spirit. Many of the cultural design limitations were eased or removed in our relating. We expanded our spirits as we explored ourselves in Mexico, had room service, had strawberries in bed, and gave ourselves and each other permission and encouragement to be the wholest/fullest spirits in physical form we could be at the time. It was wonderful."

When we met on May 8, 1970, Jim was a national accounts sales manager with a large automotive parts manufacturing company near Detroit, Michigan. He and his first wife were in the process of divorce at the time. Then, in the late summer of that year, he quit his job and came to California, transferring his math and engineering skills into the financial planning business world that was evolving in southern California. We were married in Palm Springs on October 30, 1970.

During the course of his second writings the Memorial Day weekend of 1999, Jim rolled the tape of his life through our years together in southern California, through the ten years we were in northern California, and through the period when we moved back to his home state of Michigan in 1986 to finish our studies for the book we had in process. Back to the heartland of America, we said at the time.

He then wrote about his life up to 1998 when his "iron man" father became seriously ill with the last stages of pancreatic cancer, from which he passed on within two weeks. Jim had helped his mother take his father home from the hospital and had stayed with his parents at their home for most of the two weeks his father was in the process of leaving this life. Jim wrote, "This passing returned me into direct relationship with my parents, and with my mother and the life we shared and share."

Jim's mother was eighty-seven when his father passed on. Since Jim was an only child, he became actively and directly involved with her and all the resulting details set into motion when his father died, which included her health problems. Therefore, after his father's passing Jim had been driving back and forth across the state from our home in southwestern Michigan to his mother's home in the southeastern part of the state, while continuing his business and community focuses. It wasn't long before he realized he no longer would have time for most of his volunteer activities of board affiliations and committee memberships. But obviously those deletions weren't enough because he developed severe abdominal pains with periodic eruptions of hives all over his body. After the third dramatic episode, we decided we would deal even more directly with the cause.

Since Jim's mother had emphatically refused to move to our area and become part of our lives there, insisting her very identity was tied up in the community where she lives and in the land and home she and Jim's father had built upon it forty-three years before, Jim and I decided to move across the state to Ann Arbor. This seemed to me to be what we should be doing as I deeply and consistently sought divine guidance. And I want to add that I think it was a really good decision and move for all of us.

We easily found a vacant townhouse in a lovely rental complex, with two bedrooms downstairs and an upstairs loft suite. Jim moved his business operations—insurance, investments, and retirement and estate planning—into the second downstairs bedroom, and I took the upstairs area.

Jim's second writing over the 1999 Memorial Day weekend continued with him looking at his being brought back into direct relationship with his mother, his past as a growing child, and how it all related to the crisis he was in during the past week. He wrote, "Even though it is all based in a very deep love, it has brought forth all the cultural designs my parents represent and overloaded my circuits. Overall, that is O.K. It is desirable. It is an opportunity to bring everything up to date in the present and make whatever modifications I need to make in my designs. This is the process that has been going on for the past several months, which has come to a crisis point during the past week into the present."

He next looked at all the people and emphases he currently has in his life, coming to the conclusion, "My spiritual needs are very large at this time." He finished his second writing in the series of four by stating he and I need to seek and achieve spiritual health, and everything else will fall into place. This is along with what needs to be done from day to day.

In his third writing Jim went through more memories. The following is the full text of his fourth writing, the summary and his conclusion on May 31, 1999.

"I feel it has been suitable and fitting I have been remembering and summarizing my life and being during this Memorial Day weekend in what is considered to be the ending year of the 20th century. My life has been unconventional in that it hasn't been lived within the confines of cultural conventions as a true believer, even though I have come to understand the cultural designs and agreements very well in recent years and am very skilled in a cultural sense.

"What I have sought throughout my life is to become the person I want and choose to be. I started out by trying to fit myself into the roles and ways of being my culture and its members said I should adopt. It seemed like whatever I did in

those terms resulted in experiences which were both good and
bad, contained a spectrum of emotions and emotional conflict,
and for the most part led down a road into a kind of cul-de-sac
of relationships that really didn't seem to be enriching or good for
anyone. There were always winners and losers, problems and
difficulties, and lots of dissatisfaction. Including my own. In
addition, my life and the lives of many others seemed so
unfulfilled and depressed. A struggle. A dead end. I needed to
find another way of being—Something Different.

"That was true even before I met Jacquie. In fact, it has been
true all my life. I have been seeking a way of life which is not limited by cultural limitations. Now, I would not have done this if the
designs of the culture I adopted in my earlier years had worked
and had led to a satisfying life. I approached my marriage with my
first wife and the birth of the children with enthusiastic hopes and
dreams. But it never even came close. The designs we learned from
our culture to use to be male and female, husband and wife,
parents and children, and to be in relationship with the cultural
world around us, included heavy doses of competition rather than
loving cooperation—dooming us from the beginning.

"I know that by the end of my first marriage and my time in
the cultural corporate structure, I was completely fed up with the
whole thing and with life in general as I knew it at the time. This
led to the next phase of my life and to my coming together with
Jacquie, where we joined our quests and evolved ourselves into
who we are today.

"So going on from here is the current-day focus. I do not
avoid confrontation but I do not seek it. What I seek is

enriching, enhancing relationships which are truly beneficial for everyone. Ones in which the participants create a sense of love and caring for one another at no one else's expense, and they can be themselves as the fundamental free spirits they are as much as possible. This applies to my relationship with myself and Jacquie, my relationship with my mother, and my relationship with everyone I meet and know, including all business associations. Mutually beneficial relationships in all ways."

Shortly after Jim completed his writings, he began to feel better.

Original Grandeur

This snapshot came forth as raw materials before Jim's Memorial Day weekend crisis. I think it correlates with some of what he wrote regarding his life experiences. During his crisis he told me, "Males are not any more immune to abuse than females are. They may not know it, but they aren't." He was stating that underneath all the tough training, guys do get hurt and do suffer!

One of Jim's continued emphases has been upon being valued. *I think not being valued as the fundamental being each of us is starts each child's pain. It seems to me when children do not feel their basic worth and oftentimes are devalued with coercion tactics, they begin to develop protective coping devices, which continue on into adulthood.*

From my viewpoint, over the years many males exchange being valued and valuing themselves as fundamental spirit for cultural adulations in the form of sports accomplishments, money-making and power-over-others performances. Alongside of this, a female can get cultural validation from being a mother and wife, from the man she is with, from her looks and sexuality, and from her own accomplishments that are similar to those of males. *Nevertheless, I think there is a hole in one's soul, a craving for something that should be one's birthright that no cultural accomplishment can completely fill as a substitute.*

Many people have talked about psychological-emotional defenses and physical body armor, which I believe at the beginning are the results of children developing ways to protect themselves from various and varying cultural expectations and onslaughts. Then, they are added to over the course of one's life.

I believe many people have experienced themselves at deeper levels but afterward have not known what to do with their experiences and feelings. This explains to me why some people start thinking about themselves as being God or some other grandiose picture of themselves. *I think it is very difficult to translate these expanded levels into a culture that only officially recognizes one level of existence.*

In December last year, I wrote a poem expressing some of this viewpoint:

TRANSLATING ORIGINAL GRANDEUR

There has been many
   a soul
Who has intuitively sensed
   his or her potential grandeur.
And then in the translation
   into this cultural reality,
Something happened.
Many things happened.
And something more happened.

When grandeur is translated
    through opposites and oppositions,
    it is burned up in conflicts.
There's lots of heat and action.

When grandeur is translated
    into dominance and superiority,
It follows there are those
    who are diminished
    and made to feel worthless
While others become
    inflated and self-important.

When one asks oneself—
What happened to my original grandeur?
The answer comes back—
Something happened to it
    in the translation.

Belonging

My own experiences and observations of other people have shown me that no matter what social class, religious group, and ethnic heritage one is part of, there are strong motivations to fit in, or at least to not be outside what the group expects from its members. In a culture where invisible core patterns of dualism and superiority/inferiority are operating, within many groups there is a built-in way of thinking to be protective of one's own group, which oftentimes includes being against other groups. Rather than giving an example at this moment, I invite readers to think about their own lives and experiences from this perspective.

In my life, I find myself being sensitive to the nuanced expectations to be one of the girls, whatever that means to the group I am with. The expectations include a myriad of patterns such as who we are said to be as females, who males are said to be, and how it is all said to work in general.

And what if one doesn't fit in? How are individuals ostracized by others? One way is to assume an attitude of disdain toward the offending member, sometimes calling that person "weird" or "crazy." Guys will call other guys a "girl" or "sissy," said with an emotional tone of contempt. Girls oftentimes put one another down for not being fashionable enough or for other reasons like being too smart.

Valuing mental activities can bring about problems for individuals in relationship with the group they belong to or want to belong to. I think there have been two themes in our society about using one's intelligence. The first has been used extensively by immigrants and others who value knowledge and its skillful application. It says the way to move up in the world is through hard work and education.

The second theme has been one of anti-intelligence. There are current-day categories like "hunks" and "nerds," "nerds" being the guys who are smart but not oriented toward physical activities. When I was growing up, we were told in multiple ways that it wasn't in a female's best interest to be intelligent. My experience was there were many males who wanted me to be a pretty head and body, and a pleasant person to be with. But to go much beyond that, with ideas of my own that didn't fit with theirs, was not what they wanted from me.

Many of us have carefully walked some fine lines throughout our lives, wanting to keep our group and cultural memberships while also being the individuals we have known we could be. Oftentimes, compromises have been made, most of them at an unconscious or semi-conscious level.

I think one of the ways we have been controlled by others, and how we have controlled ourselves and others, is by holding an active belief that if a person hears internal voices, he or she is crazy. I think this pattern came from our scientific descriptions of what is said to be real and what isn't—that only what can be experienced with the physical five senses is real.

I believe each of us already belongs to a group in a spirit sense, like there is a vast spirit family, and now we each have the opportunity to expand and translate this understanding and membership into our individual lives of today.

Protections and Their Replacements

One of the pictures becoming clearer to me is that as we live our lives from early childhood, we develop portions of our adult worldviews in particular ways because we believe we need protections in order to survive in this cultural system. Then, oftentimes these become automatic defenses with which we view our worlds, react to others, and cocreate events with fellow human beings.

Jim tells me some of the common protections he learned from our society were "the best defense is a good offense," aggressiveness, anger, hurt, and inaccessibility.

The protections I learned were a mix of designs. My father believed fears and cautions were safety measures. From an early age, I devised a protection of usually keeping my most controversial opinions and decisions about life to myself. Looking back now, I know there were many culturally sanctioned patterns I refused to use because I had an inner feeling I would someday figure out a way to do things that felt really good to me. I also believed certain kinds of knowledge give one personal power, which could be used in healthy ways as a type of strength and protection.

A few years ago, I was in a place in my life where visual symbols emerged from my psyche—sometimes in dreams and sometimes when I would begin to go into or come out of meditation. One such symbol was that of an onion. When I experienced it, I knew it represented the need for me to peel off additional layers, many of them including patterns of self-protection. Recently, I have been doing just that—peeling off more layers of my protective devices, becoming much more open.

It's totally clear to me now that when I developed these protections throughout my life, *I did so within different contexts.* The framework I consciously lived within did not have the underlying and expansive divinity within which I currently live my life, nor its basic safety. In those earlier years, I also hadn't formed the replacement patterns I now have developed for the ones I had absorbed from my culture.

As I see it, these understandings of who and what I am and what my real home is have now flowed to some degree throughout all the layers of my being. Therefore, the automatic protective processes I developed are becoming integrated and washed with that reality. More than likely, many of their energies have been and are being transformed.

It was exciting the other day when I realized I am more open now. I also think I can be more in the present than I have ever been before. At the same time, if it's appropriate to engage in some type of protective energetic dance, I can do that as well. There are specific situations where I carefully evaluate the wisdom of using those designs. In other words, I certainly am able to protect myself if an occasion seems to call for it. I don't feel at all impotent—I feel alive!

Verbal and Written Communication—Words

For decades, my intention with both verbal and written communication has been to describe situations, experiences, thoughts, and emotions as clearly as I can, with the language I have to work with. Because I was so focused upon my quest of accurate word descriptions, for years it continued to amaze me when others were not attempting to do similar things. There have been many times in my life when I took what people said as their intent, expecting their actions to match their words, when in fact they were using communication for different purposes.

Hurray. I think I finally have the picture clear now, all the way to my bones. Each of us uses words in our own ways for our own purposes, and in different ways at different times.

Words can be used to cover, hide, and distort. They can be used to purposely deceive others. They can be used, especially with accompanying emotional tones, to control and dominate. Words can be used to get sympathy or attention. They can be used to entertain, mesmerize, or enchant others. They can be used to shock people. They also can be used to describe ideas, situations, experiences, and events as clearly as one is capable of doing.

It is with a considerable amount of relief I now can say I think I am usually able to listen to what someone says with openness and without skepticism, while at the same time hearing some of the patterns he or she is using. I can then see how the person's actions and life events match up with what he or she says. I also factor in to a considerable extent how I feel when I am with a person.

During my recent time-out, one of my focuses was upon activating more of my right brain—the nonverbal part that is musical, poetic, associative, sees pictures, and has overall awareness. I was highly sensitized to being fully present to the experiences I was having, without thinking with words. I purposely set them off to the side as best I could. Therefore, my experiences were often like unfolding processes of discovery. I think my logical and language-using left brain observed with interest but made no comment. It has had enough experience by now to know that when it eventually comes into the act, it has a big part to play. After a while when the time seemed appropriate, I would ask myself how to accurately describe the experience, and a flow would come forth.

One of my goals is to harmoniously blend all my processes and capacities, where I use complementary designs in place of either/or limitations. I see all of this in terms of living my life as an artist, like playing around with color and brush strokes, where when I pay attention to the layers of my being there is usually an overall sense of what to do and when to do it.

I think sharing our lives with one another, using words verbally or in writing, in a sincere back and forth flow of conversation, can result in healthy mental, emotional, and spiritual connections. Of course this picture includes the patterns each person is using and what emotions she or he is communicating.

The Languages of Emotions and Intuitive Feelings

The forthcoming snapshot emerged from developments after my time-out focuses and experiences.

In addition to the language of words, from my perspective emotions are a type of language, used all the time in communication with oneself and others. In basic terms, I think emotions are part of our human equipment, to be used by each of us as an internal feedback system. They are also used as messengers of communication between our species and other species. They are internal and external signals, symbols, and attention-getters. Moreover, as I understand it, beliefs, thoughts, and emotions strongly affect our body's neurochemicals.

About thirty years ago, I came to the conclusion that emotional feelings such as jealousy and envy of others were signals for me to pay attention, to ask myself what was missing in my life that I was seeing in someone else's, and then to set about bringing that to myself.

If I experience what is culturally called anger, I let the energies arise within me to possibly use if appropriate for action, but first I relanguage the feelings to myself as heat, meaning there is energy there that has been aroused. I also pause because underneath this heat are usually feelings such as hurt, sadness, resentment, frustration, rejection, and impotence. In other words, there is more going on.

If disappointment comes forth, I have the opportunity to look at what hopes, dreams, or expectations I was originating and to then decide whether it is a good idea to continue with those emphases or to choose another path.

I have learned that when disturbing emotional feelings are allowed to flow freely as I pay attention to them, something wonderful happens. It can be the recognition of a change or changes I need to make, a conversation I need to have with someone, or just the movement of emotions and thoughts for the purpose of conscious awareness. Obviously, I have channels of communication within myself that are well-established, thanks to the therapist/consultant I went to when I was in the process of separation and divorce in the late 1960s. He constantly focused my attention on my emotional here and now. I also did a lot of practicing by asking myself, "What's happening at this moment?"

In addition to letting emotions flow freely, I have concluded it's usually a good idea to add words to the experience. I mean easily describing to myself what I am experiencing as accurately as I can, without smothering it with language. In so doing I am able to be clearer and gain perspective about what's happening and where I am in my life. Writing in my journal has also been and is very therapeutic and clarifying.

Summarizing my own experiences and observations about fear, I find that it always limits and contracts, which gives it short-term value for emergency actions. But using it as a foundation pattern is another matter. Studies show that when people experience joy, contentment, or love, they think more broadly and are more open to new ways of thinking.

For years I have been specifically identifying my fears, worries, and anxieties, thanking them for the cultural protection they have given me. Then when appropriate, I have replaced them with thoughtfully chosen spirit patterns, such as living my life amidst a wavelength of divine love, trust, joy, and ease, where what happens is within the matrix of what is in my highest good and the highest good of all life everywhere, factoring in the context of our current-day industrialized world.

Emotions as I understand them are also the fire of desire, the fuel for creativity. I have heard it said that emotions combined with imagination are the most concentrated forms of energy in this system. In terms of effectiveness, I would add the elements of clear choices, purposeful intent, wavelength, consistency, and follow-through.

Along with relationships, we females were given emotions in general in the cultural division that took place long ago for males and females. And have we ever had a lot to keep track of as we've lived our lives within our cultural emotional pattern complexes! Males, on the other hand, have been relentlessly programmed to hide their feelings, where oftentimes they are hidden even from themselves. The emotional exception has been anger and its variations. As far as other emotions are concerned, I have heard men say it sometimes takes a day or two for them to know what they are feeling and to then process with the feelings.

When reading what men write and listening to them talk, a consistent theme I have heard is how shame and belittlement were used almost continuously in their lives to get them to conform to who they were supposed to be. In fact, a picture I now have is that male *fear of shame* is a huge controller of their behavior and their internal self-awareness. Therefore, they want to avoid feeling shame at all costs!

Shaming was also a method my father used to try to control me. He would intensely tell me with a great deal of verbal force how much I should be ashamed of myself for some infraction by me, from his point of view. I can still remember the horrible visceral responses I would have in the midsection of my body. Interestingly, I just realized I have never asked anyone else what shaming felt like to them. I think more than likely I didn't want to talk about it.

As I understand cultural matters, guilt is closely connected to shame. Now I happen to believe there is a natural guilt one feels deep inside when one betrays oneself and others as spirit in basic ways, a feeling of unease or discord. But cultural guilt is often used to control people, to get them to play the part someone else wants them to play. I think natural guilt can be used as a valuable motivating energy to make substantial changes in oneself and one's life, whereas cultural guilt is oftentimes manipulative, and I question its more basic value.

One of the delightful results occurring during the past twenty-some years in my life is that my emotions have changed. By not personally fueling dualisms or superiority/inferiority, I don't experience highs and lows in pendulum swing terms. My usual emotional state is like a steady hum or purr, with variations. At times I experience some beautiful emotional feelings that aren't really describable in cultural ways. And now, when disturbing emotions come forth, I'm even more welcoming of them as indications of what else is going on, giving me increasing clarity and potency.

Many people seem to believe if they don't experience recurring crisis dramas, their lives will be dull and boring. I've known some women who seem to seek out highly charged emotional events. Nevertheless, if a person chooses to explore dramas of a different kind, I would suggest consciously playing around with removing all dualisms in one's life as an experiment for a couple of months and see what happens. This should begin to put him or her on another wavelength, if done consistently and effectively. Of course before doing that, he or she would have to figure out what the dualisms are and which ones are being used personally.

Some examples of cultural dualisms are given throughout this book. They include opposites and oppositions such as us against them, and winning or losing. Examples of emotional dualisms are sadness and joy, anger and placating, grouchiness and sunniness, and aggressiveness and passiveness. Oftentimes, a person will connect with someone who is playing out the other part in the dualism to what the first person is setting forth.

From my point of view, it is an excellent idea to allow disturbing emotions and images from one's past to come into the present, thereby seeing the past from a current-day perspective. One can do what needs to be done with what emerges in order to free up energies to be used differently. At the very least, more options would be available. A technique I've used, after looking at the past matrixes each of us individually was operating from in a situation, is to then infuse divine love and understanding into the whole event at the soul level. I can tell if I've been effective with the process by how I feel afterward, when I purposely think about that scene again.

Then there are *intuitive feelings* with their own language, which for me are different than emotional feelings. Some of them are in the realm of internal feeling tones I describe as a sense of right-on-ness, of inner bells, and chords of harmony. They are closely associated with divine guidance and primarily come from my guts. There is also what I would call a *deep and direct knowing.* That is, I just *know.*

Some of these internal intuitive feelings come about from what I believe is an invisible communication network amongst ourselves as human beings and with members of other species. As I understand how it works, a person's interpretation of these inner messages depends upon the thought and emotion patterns he or she uses.

Taking the time to listen, and learning how to listen to these multiple inner communications, has been essential for me in terms of choosing what to do and not do in my life. I also follow up, when it seems appropriate, to find out how my intuition and subsequent actions correlate with what happens with other people and events, in the present and future.

A Direct Experience of the River of Love

While reading the newspaper one Sunday morning during my time-out, I suddenly felt a large wave of love coming forth from deep within me, flowing up through my heart and the rest of my body, and out toward Jim. It was an unmitigated flow of love, love without cultural form, love in one of its primal expressions. In the next instant I realized this was happening because there was not any "stuff " standing in its way. I had become current with myself and Jim within the past few days. Also, I had become even clearer.

It was wonderful—one of those glorious moments of experience in the physical world. I breathed in deeply as this energy flowed like water into all the nooks and crannies of my being. I knew it as a moment of integrating health.

A few weeks later I read a description of love from the world-view of a healer. He said there is a divine gateway that opens and you experience what unconditional love is, and it has absolutely nothing to do with conditional love emptied of all conditions. What he said was another way of describing my experience that Sunday morning while reading the paper. There were no issues or needs for protection operating at that moment in time and space. From its depth, the river of love was flowing openly and freely.

I have heard a beautiful expression from somewhere that the present is a gift if one chooses to live one's life that way. This is why it is called the present. For me, that moment in my life was an irreplaceable gift, which is now a continuing energy of memory.

Caught Between the Worlds

The author of one of the books I read recently, a noted expert in her field of mind-body connection, stated that one of the most compelling behavioral models of depression is based on feelings of helplessness.

Surely, feelings of impotence, helplessness, and resignation about facets of our lives have been rampant in our stories as females, because we were often trapped in our lives for various reasons. But Jim's recent illness, the book we read about male depression, and his writings over the Memorial Day weekend have all combined to give me a much wider screen on which to see and understand these emotional states than I have had before.

The depression that appears to be underlying many male lives today seems to have similar causes to that of females. They too are stuck in the cultural roles our society has assigned to them. Oftentimes they too feel helpless, hopeless, and resigned to their fates while their natural and underlying flow of life energy is being compressed and repressed. *What I think is being compressed and repressed is one's life force in its original form.*

Moreover, since today's almost instant global communications are now showing us what is taking place around the world—

pictures oftentimes depicting scenes of destitution and destruction—people can feel impotent and depressed about the overall magnitude of problems. I know I have felt that way in the past. In the present, I continue to be affected by what is happening to other people all over the globe.

From my personal experiences and observations, I think an emotional state can be a centerpoint for internal attractions, where one's thoughts, memories, and associated emotions align with similar contents, forming an overall composite reality.

Jim had needed a way to think about what he was experiencing emotionally. He told me, "Now that I know I was depressed, I've been able to do something about it." He began to have more of what he called substantial fun, but it wasn't enough. His next step was to realize he was still caught between the worlds as he termed it, caught between the designs of being spirit and the designs of the culture.

When he was able to conceptualize and give appropriate language to what was happening, he felt much more empowered. Nevertheless, he is continuing to wrestle with how to integrate his worlds effectively and how to translate himself forth as spirit in his life of today.

Even though it has been easier to start off by thinking about ourselves as spirit, as Jim and I both have done, there still has been the reality of effective pattern changing. I see the necessity for each person to play with his or her own life to find out what is there in the first place and then to experiment, developing processes that lead to more joy and continual evolvement.

Belief Structures

M any large-scale belief structures are based upon the sincerely held assumption that they are accurately and completely describing the story of how *everything* works. *My perspective is no matter how expansive a belief structure, it is still a belief structure, one among many other valid maps that are also available to be used and experienced. I think each structure provides a container and/or a framework for personal and group experiences.*

Over the years I have heard, read, and played around with my own versions of many belief structures, also called worldviews. During my recent time-out I read descriptions of three large ones I was not aware of before—one from Asia, one from Mexico, and one from the United States. I also read a fourth one—an updated interpretation by an American of some Hindu Yogic beliefs.

There were valuable perspectives for me within each of them, ways of thinking about life I hadn't heard expressed just that way before. When I incorporated and blended elements and understandings from them that seemed healthy to include into my worldview at this time, I felt more expanded and actually changed.

At the same time, the central construct in my worldview I formed years ago still makes the most sense to me. Summarizing, I continue to see each of us as basically spirit, a part of God and somehow interrelated with all spirit. I believe at the spirit level there are models and patterns for all probable experiences in this reality system. They are probabilities until we as spirit-people energize them. I also believe each of us as a human being is a pattern maker, user, and experiencer in this system. This is part of the deal and how it all works. Then as God experiences Itself through all our combined experiences and choices, I see It as fluid and in motion, not static.

Therefore, we as individualized portions of God play our parts by breathing life into various combinations of patterns through the use of our God-given powers. In addition, I see each of us as spirit-people having the opportunity to use another of our God-given powers, which is to specifically choose the patterns we are going to energize and to actualize them in our own unique ways.

Recently, I heard there is a question being asked in academic circles: How free are we really? Are we kidding ourselves when we think we are acting freely when in fact we are acting out of our own individualized cultural programming? Then there are those who would say our cultural training and educations are in order to teach us all we need to know about Reality.

Along the lines of the question of how free are we really, I was recently affected by a portion of the writings of the man who was born in Mexico, mentioned earlier. His perspective was that all of us have emotionally wounded bodies and most humans see the world through their emotional poisons. The way to handle this, he says, is to go into the wounds, cleaning them of all the accumulated poisons through a process of self-honesty and self-love. One forgives others for what one experienced as injustices, thus freeing oneself. As I see it, his description is a process where a person can then realign with her or his own essence, understanding and reframing her or his life, extracting its value and one's own value as spirit.

In the late 1970s, when Jim and I were living in northern California, I experienced a large-scale dream that has served as a way of thinking at times for myself and others over the past twenty-some years. As I reflected and played with the dream afterward, I called it "Bands of Reality." In the dream, I as my essence was taken out of this system so I could see it from a distance, from behind it and a little above it. It was like there were bands of reality that I later called bands D, C, B, and A. I was in band D, which was at the spirit level. The next band, C, was the whole construction of the earth system and its subsequent evolution of which we humans are a part—the waters, the land, the air, the seasons, night and day, the sun, the moon, and all species on the earth, including their interrelationships. Since time and space are included in the design, there are distances and distinct separations that spread it all out.

Then from my position in band D, there were two bands after band C. Bands B and A were brought into existence by us humans, as our ancestors and ourselves have played roles as the users, constructors and experiencers of the beliefs, concepts, emotions, significances, and intents each of us energizes.

Band B was where the solid citizens lived their lives most of the time, but since there usually was more vitality and vividness in band A, there were many temptations for band B participants to cross over and be more than spectators in relationship with band A.

In my dream I was being shown how the human-constructed patterns for bands B and A are easily replaceable when one understands the process and puts in the effort to make the changes.

At this point you might be asking if there were any guides with me on the dream trip I took. To the best of my recollection, there were no distinct presences. And at the same time, I was aware of an overall wise and loving guidance throughout the whole experience, where I felt totally safe.

In another dream in the late 1970s, I was in what I called band D, looking toward this physical system. What I saw was a culturally constructed ring of fear surrounding the earth system, keeping people from experiencing directly the divine spirit level. The ring of fear itself was filled with opposites and oppositions, distorting the direct potential of cooperative interaction we humans are capable of having with others. I also saw these dualisms burning up energies as they played out, without actually going anywhere. They were part of bands B and A. The "Ring of Fear" dream came at a time when I was beginning to purposely remove many of my own dualistic programs, while replacing them with unified patterns I could use directly with others when appropriate.

As far as I am concerned, this picture I am painting of bands of reality and the ring of fear is not capital R reality. They are both mental constructs I have used along the way that have been helpful to me in terms of my journey and process. In the present, Jim and I both use bands of reality to think with at various times.

During my years of searching for clarity and understanding, I've read about and played with my own version of many large-scale belief structures or parts of them. In my opinion, several of the structures said to describe how it all works have been intelligently and lovingly fashioned. Their authors present a vision designed to answer all questions, some even having a big mystery as part of the overall construction. Nevertheless, my experience is that in many cases these turn out to be one reality enclosed systems, whereas I think the whole thing is much more open, flexible, and potentially individual.

Wavelengths

This is another snapshot from my two-month time-out in May and June 1999. It seemed to be asking for its own emphasis rather than being amongst other thoughts and ideas.

For the present, I am concluding that the combination of one's beliefs, emotions, interests, significances, and intents intermingle to bring about a vibrational wavelength within which one then operates, from which one makes connections with others and then experiences the results. When I take the time to reflect, I can tell what wavelength I'm within by my thoughts and feelings at that moment. *I know a divine love wavelength is filled with joy.* Certainly, the wavelength a person operates within fluctuates during the day and night.

I think because so much of our culture is filled with fear, many people are experiencing the results of being amidst a fear frequency much of the time. My experiences are it is a heavy frequency, and people within it at times feel depressed or semi-depressed. I believe the accumulating pictures of violent images people have seen on television, in movies, videos, video games, and news reports contribute to this situation.

For a long time now, I have been playing with the question of how to be kindly and compassionately in relationship with others who are using culturally based designs that oftentimes contain fear, while at the same time seeing things clearly and not getting caught up in their dramas in unhealthy ways.

What I have been discovering is the very best place for me to be stationed as much as possible is at the spirit level where fresh divine guidance, strength, love, and safety are always available. This is a place I believe is available to us all. From this position, I think by seeing others basically as spirit, one connects with and strengthens that dimension of them, even though consciously they may not be aware of it. This is in contrast with getting hooked emotionally into the wavelengths of others and whatever they may contain, because for some reason one wants to be accepted by them or thinks this is how it has to be in order to be empathetic and loving.

All of this is in experimental stages. At present, sometimes when I feel myself becoming emotionally entangled in unhealthy ways, I plunge deeply into divine love and trust and let the rest of it move on. I continue this focus until a shift takes place. From my experiences and observations, gratitude in the moment for what a person has in her or his life—and for life itself—can also raise one's wavelength.

About a year ago, one evening before going to sleep, Jim and I were harmonizing our energies by meditating together. During the meditation process I felt myself as my essence begin to ascend higher and higher. Now for decades I had always gone deeply down and within for many reasons. One reason was that I had seen how easily people, in my opinion, had intermixed beliefs of ascending spiritual levels with cultural patterns of superiority and elitism.

So there I was that night, ascending right through my own vertical ceiling! I was both amused and excited. When I was telling a friend who has meditated for decades about my vertical ascent, as contrasted with going to my usual depth, he sounded most skeptical as he wondered aloud about my seeing myself in some superior way. This all set me to wondering if superiority/inferiority ranking, which goes on almost continuously in the lives of males, may be one of the most difficult patterns for them to remove from their automatic thought processes. Obviously, in my own life I had been avoiding the whole issue when I refused to go in a vertical direction.

After my vertical ascent experience, I began to play around with both ascent and descent in terms of positioning myself at the spirit level. Then over the past few months, I've been divinely advised to expand out in all directions. One day it was like the connections were made between depth, breadth, and height. I experienced that when I went very deeply, I could move around circularly on the same wavelength in all directions!

Nonembodied Beings and Reincarnation

After Jim's Memorial Day weekend crisis, including the writings he did in order to move through it, I asked him if I could use portions of what he had written and he agreed. We decided to call it "Jim's Odyssey," and it appears earlier in this section. An aftermath was he strengthened the desire that had been building over time to express himself more fully.

His next step was to buy paperback copies of Homer's *The Iliad* and *The Odyssey* because he had a sense of connection with that time and place. From Jim's point of view, they laid out what people in ancient Greece believed and thought about life in general, representing many of their imaginings and life experiences. He saw the designs within those representations as being part of our cultural heritage. Some were patterns he had incorporated into his day-to-day ways of doing things from his family and community experiences, especially beliefs about personal power in relationship with others, athletics, and competition. That is, until he changed many of his operating designs. Now he was seeking even further clarity.

From my point of view, the patterns Jim was talking about were part of the big cauldron at the soul level I discussed in "Spirit and Soul."

Jim's new focus put us both back in certain ways into Homer's mythological stories of ancient Greeks and Trojans who believed in nonembodied gods and goddesses. These events set off a chain of thoughts and associations for me regarding beliefs about non-embodied beings.

Back in the late 1970s, a young woman who had been living on the east coast of the United States moved to our area in northern California. She graciously let me read books she had brought with her that were called esoteric, that is, containing knowledge kept hidden and passed on to only a select few in previous ages. Most of what they were saying was new to me. In them I found all sorts of assumptions about astral planes and nonembodied beings that were not attractive to me. I remember mentally telling myself, "I'm not doing this." After awhile, I felt the same way about Carlos Casteneda's fascinating accounts of his adventures in Mexico with don Juan Matus, a man who came out of the shamanic tradition. Carlos characterized don Juan as a Yaqui Indian sorcerer. My interpretation of what I was reading was that they went strongly into fear, which I decided to not do.

Looking back at that period, what I now realize is that divine guidance was advising me I didn't even need to play around in those realms. Instead, it said I could go to a deeper and more harmonized level of being, the roots of my being, which I also heard were part of the roots of everyone's being. This is the design I used over and over and over again. There were many occasions when I would count back slowly from ten to zero as I descended to this place I was calling the roots of my being, in order to explore what was there and to immerse myself in its environment. It was there I learned about divine love directly. From today's viewpoint, I was into what I now know as the spirit level. My process worked well. During all my years of inner exploration, I have never had an unpleasant experience.

In my opinion, in order to access some of the wonder and expansiveness of our lives, it is necessary to think about levels and layers to one's being. This way, a person can understand how at a certain level one is living in time and space, while in another dimension it is a timeless reality. The challenge is how to effectively translate and integrate it all.

In all honesty, I don't know how to think about some of the earth-oriented nonembodied beings people describe as spirits who communicate with them, other than to see them as still connected to our earth system or else wanting to be connected to it through humans who currently live here. One of the patterns I use is to only go as far with mental constructs and thought processes as I am able to go with a certain type of clarity. Otherwise, I begin to feel ungrounded. So, this is as far as I am able to go at present.

My conclusion continues to be that what are called evil spirits somehow come about in one's life through emphases of fear, jealousy, hate, and frozen anger such as resentment. I think all the thoughts and emotions each of us sets forth have both a form and an energetic charge that connects us with like-minded energies. I also think we do not need to be afraid of nonembodied beings if we choose to operate within divine love wavelengths.

The bottom line to what I am saying here is that I believe there are many belief structures one can choose from to form the containers or frameworks for one's experiences. I think the choice is really up to each of us.

Reincarnation is a concept used extensively in Hindu and other belief constructions around the globe. For some people, reincarnation means they have lived other lives and in this life are paying prices and/or reaping rewards for what they have done or not done in previous lives. For other people who believe in a larger sense all time is really simultaneous, reincarnation means they are living other lives simultaneously to the one they now experience, where there is a flow of effects between the lives.

While Jim and I were doing our tours through history, we both played around with feelings of connections we had to certain times, places, and people who lived in earlier eras. I used it as a way to see aspects of myself more clearly.

My choice continues to be to focus in the present. Certainly it could be that I have other lives. I don't know, and it really doesn't matter because I think it is up to me to get things as right as I can in *this* life. The way I look at it is that if I affect possible other lives of mine elsewhere, that's fine, and anything that might be coming my way from them I can take care of in the present. By focusing my energies into this life, I believe I am more responsible, less diffused, and hence have more potency.

Moreover, I think some of the belief constructions I am aware of regarding reincarnation are of the kind I described earlier in

"Belief Structures"—fairly enclosed systems designed to fully describe how it all works, whereas in actuality they each may be one of many valid ways to organize energies within forms, and to then have experiences within that framework.

From the spirit level, I think God can speak to us freshly in many ways. There are times someone will say something, where an inner chord will go off telling me it is just what I need to hear. Or there will be a book that comes into my life, a magazine article, a newspaper report, or something I hear on the radio that also rings sounds of inner responses. Then there are always dreams and other inner pictures. In addition, I do personally believe there are messengers that come directly from God, called "angels" in our culture, who assist us humans. There are times I have a sense of a divine presence in the room with me. I have realized, in addition to divine guidance always being available, divine assistance is available when requested.

Personal Power, Potency, and Freedom

Personal power and potency has been one of the themes and issues in my life. The first dream I remember as a child was one in which I was an infant in my high chair in the kitchen. In my dream I was kidnapped by a couple and was unable to make any sound to call for help. Then I grew up as a female, which in those years was a one-down position. Along with that I was a small-framed female.

About a year ago I had lunch with a friend who is a very creative and artistic person. She lives her life with a lot of zest and flair. We had scarcely been seated when she excitedly told me she had dreamed about the two of us the night before. In the dream we had been in Chicago—having what she said was a high old time—when an older man with a hat on his head began to follow us and act in menacing ways. This continued for quite a while until we found refuge in the yard of a home on the street where we were walking. My friend shook her head as she said, "I didn't know what to make of it."

While she had been relating her dream story, some of the symbols immediately and strongly resonated with me, which was quite interesting. My personal interpretation was the older man in the hat represented our past-present cultural agreements that have built-in punishments that are used to keep people within the confines of the system. He was afraid we might be too mentally and emotionally free. I think he was afraid of our personal potency.

What was especially satisfying for me as I listened to the account of the dream was I felt absolutely no fear or anxiety. From my point of view, what I am doing with my writings is to open probable windows and doors for other people to use in terms of their own worldviews, as many other writers are doing in our world today. I am also doing it in such a manner that if people choose to make changes, they can do so in relatively easy and empowering ways, as contrasted with past social revolutions.

As I see it, our cultural programming on the whole has been such that each of us to some degree has been fearfully indoctrinated to think we need validation, approval, appreciation, and recognition from others for our very existence and well-being. We are trained to invest others with power by how we think about them and how we subsequently act toward them and ourselves. To my mind, one thing this "out there" orientation has done is to not give us humans an opportunity to go inside and become as whole and full as we can be, in an integrated, divine sense.

I think many forms of the type of power we have been culturally programmed to use are fundamentally quite limited—controlling and dominating others through position, emotional and intellectual intimidations or withholdings, and/or physical violence. For me, this type of power is fundamentally limited because it isn't based upon what I think is the true reality of who and what each of us is, nor upon the potentiality each person has in terms of creative options.

A few months ago, I heard an author read from his book of recollections about growing up as a male. In one of his stories, he described the teasing and tormenting he had experienced and dished out in his life, commenting that the teasing stops when the victim loses the power of resistance, when the victim's will is undone and the victor knows the feelings that go with dominance.

As I understand how it works, it is our God-given right as humans to be free to use the patterns and emphases we choose. At the same time, while there are no divine punishments, there are natural consequences that result from the choices we make, whether they are consciously or unconsciously made. I believe it's up to each person how he or she uses his or her power, potency, and freedom—and to be responsible for his or her choices.

During the process of reclaiming the power I had given over to others, I have been using an "all things considered" evaluator. After appropriate discussions with other people who are involved in the situation, I make choices based upon getting my life right in a divine sense. Then, I let what I energize go forth. Hence, as I see it, I have freed myself by playing my part in the way I feeI I should be playing it.

Freedom for me means to know what my options are for what choices I can make, including how to think and act, while at the same time understanding the ramifications my various thoughts and actions might have for myself, other humans, and other species.

Personally, I like grittiness and courageousness—a solidly based, gutsy approach to life. I also like living life as a dance, an easy flow of movement within an environment of divine love, trust, joy, ease, and beauty.

Personal power for me is a composite of knowing who and what one is, why one is here on the earth at this time, having increasing clarity about the patterns one is choosing to energize, what one's intents are, and becoming increasingly skillful at living life artfully. I think the ability to consistently translate choices and intentions into daily actions and interactions with others is crucial. The starting point for me is to know each of us has original value and to flow my life from there. Frankly speaking, I think I am at the *initial stages* of putting all these aspects together in a well-crafted manner, living my life on a daily basis with Jim as artists of the spirit.

Yes, life moves on for all of us. I believe as the human species, together we can solve current-day problems by individually seeking divine guidance and assistance while operating from different wavelengths, using patterns other than those we used to create existing difficult situations in the first place.

One sparkling morning, while walking along the shimmering Huron River, I was filled with the glowing realization that *life itself is a miracle*—the natural world of which we humans are a portion, how it all works in overall terms, and the God-given powers we humans use and can use. I have been seeing an inner, imaginative picture of the river of divine love feeding the tree of all life, where each of us has a valuable part to play in bringing forth our world of today and tomorrow.

An Update

Where Do *We* Go from Here?

Today is Tuesday, August 27, 2002. It has been almost a year since we in the United States experienced the events of 9/11/01—when two hijacked airplanes crashed into the World Trade Center's Twin Towers in New York City; one hijacked airplane crashed into the Pentagon in Arlington, Virginia, across the river from Washington, D.C.; and a fourth hijacked plane's mission was thwarted by passengers and crew members over a field in Pennsylvania. As I understand it, the hijackers believed they were following God's directions and would be rewarded in the afterlife.

I, like most other Americans, was stunned and shocked by the events. I felt as if my family, in this case my American family, had been assaulted. Then I began to pray, "God, help us *all*," setting that forth as my contribution to the unfolding developments.

From my point of view, the hijackers, and others who perpetuate these kinds of acts, are not following God's directions but instead are using their own interpretations of internalized cultural patterns. My perspective is they haven't gone deep enough, to the core of themselves, nor have they become the people they are capable of being.

The God I know now is genderless. It is an encompassing, compassionate, Loving, caring presence in my life at all times. It loves and cares about me, all people, and all species members equally. It also has given each of us humans free will to use our God-given powers of choice and energy generation.

The God I know now does not punish. Instead, each of us in relationship with others reaps the results of the combination of our choices, both those we are consciously aware of and those below the level of our conscious awareness. I believe this is one of the design attributes of our reality system.

The God I know is here to help, whenever I ask for it.

The God I know is here for everyone, and all each of us has to do is activate our awareness of Its presence. Recent scientific studies are showing that along with serial neural sequences and associative neural networks, there is a third neural process *hardwired in our brains*. It has been called the "God-spot" by some researchers, lighting up on tests when a person is in an expanded spiritual state.

This internal spiritual system is said to be unifying and expanding, as well as transforming. For quite some time now, when I meditate, I oftentimes envision it as rivers of energy flowing through the serial and associative processes in my brain and throughout my body, transforming their circuits as is appropriate. I believe this is part of God's river of love that extends throughout the universe, connecting us all here on earth.

As I continue to read about numerous people's sincere and heartfelt efforts to live meaningful lives, in ways that include helping fellow humans and other species members live healthier lives, I feel inspired and encouraged. Nonetheless, the picture I see in a

Where Do *We* Go from Here?

multidimensional sense is one where it is quite difficult to translate deeply felt visions of more harmonizing ways of being into our worldwide cultures where patterns of dualism and opposition, designs of superiority/inferiority and ranking, thought processes where one almost automatically makes either/or choices, and constructions of One Truth beliefs have been in existence for thousands of years. *I say it is quite difficult, but not impossible.*

My personal experience of the past few years has been that by starting out with the position and perspective that my *basic identity* is spirit one with God and all spirit, it has been easier than starting with any cultural designs for being human I am aware of.

Nevertheless, it has taken a lot of consistent, focused intention to continue to remove more of my own trouble-making patterns, primarily contained within process designs that had been developed over the years, while still functioning well in a world that uses them. To do this has meant I have needed to continue to expand as a self with more divine love and clear, compassionate understanding of others, seeing how the worldview each person has is of value to her or him, and to also understand how her or his life plays out from within it. This type of emphasis upon seeing "what is" as clearly as possible has been an important and valuable focus for years now. It is a different design construction with different ingredients than cultural judgementalness.

In the summer of 1999, after I finished word-processing the snapshots from the spring and completed the third section of this book, I continued to study and write. The result was a series of small essays on various subjects. Jim joined with me to extensively update ourselves about environmental realities since we last studied them in the 1980s. We also wove our current-day ecological understandings with pictures of the global economic situation and people's lives amidst it all.

This week the U.N. World Summit on Sustainable Development is taking place in Johannesburg, South Africa. It is a follow-up to the one held ten years ago in Rio de Janeiro, Brazil. There seem to be many people, including me, who are encouraged by the increasing awareness by people about various components of the current-day environmental picture. Also, since the summit in Rio de Janeiro, new studies have brought forth more precise analyses of the whole worldwide ecosystem, as well as showing more decisively how the systems—air flow, water, temperature, land, and soil—are intricately interwoven with one another and with people's lives.

Global warming, diminishing supplies of fresh water, nuclear waste, overfishing, and the continuous poisoning of the air, water, and soil are among some of the current-day concerns.

Last week in our local paper, there was a three-paragraph report about an enormous blanket of pollution stretching across southern Asia, distorting normal weather patterns. The layer of air pollution was said to be made up of ash, acids, aerosols, and other particles emitted into the atmosphere across Asia. The "cloud" was described as nearly two miles thick, extending across the most densely populated part of the world. According to a new report from the United Nations, this phenomenon could have potentially devastating effects on the economies in those areas. The cloud layer was cutting the amount of sunlight hitting the ground by as much as 15 percent, while warming lower parts of the atmosphere.

Looking at our planet, I see it really is a small world where what happens in one part affects the whole. For all our current-day prosperity and military might, we here in the United States are not immune from the degradation of our global mutual life-support system.

An inner picture that emerged to me this week when I looked into the future is one where, if we—the global human species— continue the path we have been on for quite some time, it will eventually lead to destruction. Either that, or enough of us will purposely choose another path. Yes, I do believe in this case it is an either/or choice.

The second pathway is certainly one into unknown and uncharted territories. At the same time, in my picture it offers opportunities that will continue to develop, emerge, and unfold. I see this second direction built with *all* the positive things now being set forth, such as using hydrogen power for energy, exploring wind power, conservation, the emphasis upon sustainability, and the focus upon producing and purchasing goods in one's local commu- nity in a non-exclusive fashion. Then, these can become *stepping stones* to other realities of personal and group potency—where we operate on increasingly higher wavelengths, with other options.

I also want to compassionately add that it seems to me there are millions of people whose lives are so entwined within the existing system it is more than likely that many of them will do everything they can to maintain the status quo. This is their choice, and it certainly is a valid one.

What I believe is needed are increasingly clear pictures of the components of what I have called band C, that is, the original design of the overall Earth system and its evolvement over the ages.

On occasion, Jim and I harken back to our high school chemistry classes where one dripped acid into a beaker of an alkaline solution, when all of a sudden there were one too many drops and the whole thing became acid. We wonder if this is an apt analogy to the environment. Like how much can it take until the whole thing tilts?

I'm not talking about turning to what has been termed nature worship in the past, nor am I recommending we continue the huge separation our belief patterns have engendered between ourselves as humans and the rest of the natural world. Instead, I'm suggesting we use our God-given abilities and divine internal wiring in this era of fantastic information, communication, and technology to come up with ideas which produce health-giving results. (With a sigh I am adding that this is not an endorsement for current-day genetic engineering, genetically engineered foods, or biotechnology. I think we don't have enough spirit-person maturity as individuals or as a species to wisely evaluate and use these emerging technologies. To my mind, they are part of the self-destructive pathway.)

As I mentioned earlier, I studied and wrote a series of small essays beginning in the summer of 1999. This went on for about a year. I thought they would comprise a fourth book section that I titled, "New Songs, New Stories." Then I took some time off before beginning and completing an editing process. When Jim and I sent out manuscript submission inquiries to publishers in the early months of 2001, I was pleased with some of the responses, but there were no offers to publish. Later, as I reflected upon the situation, divine guidance first advised me to spin off the fourth section, seeing it all as valuable personal process. After playing with that probability for a while, it made sense and I decided to do it. Next, I kept having an impression that the timing wasn't right. Then, by the time I received a belated book contract offer for all four sections from a mid-sized publisher, who had previously requested a copy of the whole manuscript, other events were taking place in our lives that I'll describe later. So, with sincere appreciation I declined the offer.

A portion of those fourth section writings occurred in 2000 when Jim and I decided to start a new family at the soul level, which we called the Empowered Spirit Family. As a reminder, within my worldview the soul level is where all human designs and experiences from the past and present on earth are active or potentially active.

Jim and I envisioned the Empowered Spirit Family as both a group and a way of being, where anyone and everyone can shift, without needing to give up other appropriate affiliations at the soul level and on earth. We thought, just as there are only a few core human-originated, trouble-making patterns forming the foundation out of which our global current-day past and present have emerged and evolved, their replacements can be just a few simple designs. Here are some of our suggestions:

- All of life, everyone's life, and life itself are sacred.
- All places and species members are sacred.

- No one is more special than anyone else.
- There is room for us all.
- All of us are connected in a divine sense.
- A major focus is what works for everyone.
- Since we already know the results of mixing together dualism, superiority/inferiority, automatic either/or choices, and One Truth beliefs, we are choosing to no longer energize those designs.

Now these are just suggestions. We feel no proprietary rights with the Empowered Spirit Family, nor do we see ourselves as any more significant than anyone else who chooses to belong. It's a way of being where everyone has an equally valid voice. An evaluator we use is to see how a design and all its parts plays out for the benefit of everyone involved.

During the past year, Jim and I have been focusing even more strongly on our health and personal relationship, seeing more clearly how they intertwine, *especially in emotional ways, both health-giving and health-depleting.*

Last September 2001, about a week after 9/11, Jim's mother had a series of strokes, starting a process of hospitalization and rehabilitation. Along with being involved with her, Jim also became involved in cleaning, sorting their belongings, and selling his parents' home, with some help from me.

For many years, he had experienced large amounts of stress and pressures from various sources, as had I. For him, the result was a type of physical crash last October. It motivated us both to consult a Western world physician who practices integrative medicine, a mixture of Eastern and Western modalities. Hence, to our already primarily organic food diet we added nutritional supplements and acupuncture to help balance our systems, all of which have been beneficial.

When my bone density scan in May 2002 showed there was thinning taking place in my bones, I began an at-home weight-lifting program based on studies done at Tufts University. My body has responded marvelously to progressively increased weights! Additionally, I am taking a yoga class once a week.

As I understand it, prolonged stress can set up an acidic condition in the body, where it draws calcium from the bones in an attempt to balance itself. Obviously, the answer was to remove as many stressful situations as possible while focusing on restorative, health-promoting foods and activities. I've learned that after noting my feelings appropriately when disturbing events take place, it is wise for me to ask myself and God where the opportunities are in the situation—and then to implement the answers.

Over the past months, Jim and I have become clearer about "I," "you," and "we," playing with our lives in ways where none of our personal interests and activities dominates the other person's life or takes up too much "we" space. Our experience is it takes considerable focused intent to move between I, you, and we to achieve a balance in these ways.

We both believe "we" and "us" is an entity in its own right that needs to be nourished and fed. Many nights before going to sleep we each have mentally filled our "us" and "we" container with divine love, trust, joy, and ease. I truly think these mental and emotional actions have both accumulated and blossomed.

As described earlier, for decades I believed I was here on earth at this time for specific reasons chosen before my birth. I saw myself in relationship and in concert with other spirits becoming aware of the opportunities available here, where each of us could play our parts, helping to bring about wondrous changes—and then experiencing the results. I also saw myself as spirit forming agreements with the being who later became Jim, where together we would develop new operating patterns for a male and female—and then experience those results.

One of the ingredients of the above overall structure was my belief that I had made a sacred commitment that I was fulfilling. This provided an extensive energy pathway to do what I have been doing for years, in addition to giving my life a lot of meaning. I now see it as a wonderful *stepping stone*. Then, as the events of my life and our lives unfolded, over the past months I expanded and developed a closer relationship with my portion of God. I kept inwardly hearing It ask me, "What do *you* choose?" That is, I could decide to self-publish my manuscript or not, and whatever my choice, there would be no hard feelings—only Love. This was a huge liberation! I was thrilled because obviously I had become much of the self I had been seeing as a probability, as if "there" had become "here."

After some deliberation, I decided I needed to publish my manuscript to get my life right. I also saw this needed to be a "we" decision because it would have so many consequences for both of us. Over time, Jim joined with me, stating, "*We* need to publish it." What would I have done if he had decided differently? When we were into the process, I didn't know what would have happened if that probability became our reality. I didn't hassle him or worry about it, choosing instead to leave the system open and divinely trust.

As I have recounted many times, I've been aware of a voice of inner divine guidance since 1966. Sometime this year, one evening I was disturbed about something. Soon I heard this inner voice tell me to turn it over to God, to let It take care of my concern within Its vaster dimension, and I would be advised as to how to play my part. Then, in the next moment, I inwardly heard a larger, more expanded voice saying clearly and gently, "Let me take care of it for you" to which I replied, "Gladly." From that time on I have had a closer, even more direct relationship with God, which has been priceless beyond words. Obviously, from the time I wrote the poem about my personal God, my experiences and understandings with It have grown and deepened.

In the present, Jim is no longer caught between the worlds of spirit and the requirements of our culture as he saw it. He retired from his business last December 31, 2001. The sale of the family home was completed this past March 2002. He kept an adjacent one-and-a-quarter-acre parcel that backs up to about thirty acres of woods for a nature preserve. We frequently picnic there. His mother is ninety-one years old now, living close by in a gracious and lovely assisted living facility. She, too, enjoys going out to what she calls "The Orchard," which still has a couple of apple trees on it from previous times.

Jim has been writing his life story, titling it *A Grand Adventure, The Story of My Life from a Spirit Perspective*. He's been playing golf about once a week. And he has taken a number of workshops in addition to classes in relationship with digital photography, choosing to express his desire for beauty and his love of the natural world in his photographs. I, in turn, am delighted to see our home filling up with his beautiful pictures.

We bought a canoe in August 2001, which we've taken to many lakes in our area. After that, Jim bought a kayak to take adventuring when I'm not available. We also purchased all new camping equipment recently, including updating our beloved boots and backpacks from the mid-1970s. For our first outing we camped at a nearby lake, canoeing at dusk while Jim took pictures of herons and swans in that enchanting light. The next day we canoed on another lake, with waters of emerald green. There, we pulled our canoe ashore at a backpacker's campground and ate lunch near a very old, large, majestic tree. A picture of it now hangs above the copier in Jim's room.

This past spring and summer, I took two art classes based upon concepts described in the book, *Drawing on the Right Side of the Brain* by Betty Edwards, activating more extensively the portions of my brain that are nonverbal and more global.

Currently, I am focusing on easily interweaving being involved in our relationship, completing this manuscript and self-publishing it, becoming increasingly skillful in interpreting my body's messages, figuring out what foods and activities are healthiest for my body, being appropriately involved with Jim and what he makes significant, having some personal time, playing my part in relationships with other family members and friends, and doing my share of our joint household activities.

As I see it, there are many ways to think about "we" and "us." There is a we made up of Jim and me. There is a we made up of "We the people of the United States ..." There is a we that includes all humans on earth. There is a we that encompasses all earth species, including humans. There is a we that speaks of the Empowered Spirit Family at the soul level. And there is a we that is the sum of all of us as spirit, one with God and all spirit.

Jim and I continue to energize a matrix wherein whatever happens in our lives is in our highest good and the highest good of all being everywhere. This is a design we originate on the input side of our lives and use to ponder and interpret events when they occur. It is both an initiator and an action construction.

We, like many other people in the United States after 9/11/01, are even more focused on "what really matters." What really matters to us is our relationship with God, our relationship with ourselves and each other, our relationship with fellow humans and other species members—all in an easy, loving manner.

Also, our health really matters. We think in order to be fully healthy, we need an unlimited, open, non-stressful time frame for our lives in the present and future. Therefore, how much involvement we'll have with follow-up activities with *God's River of Love* will be designed to fit with the rest of what we are doing. To my mind, I have succeeded in my goal for this book, of it being able to stand on its own two feet and grow.

We both feel really good about setting forth the ideas, pictures, and perspectives we have presented, of getting as close as we can to how we think it all works, even though our worldviews do not have exactly the same contents. I continue to energize the designs of "living my life with no regrets" and "in a divine sense, getting my life as right as I can—in all ways." From my point of view, with the publication of this word-picture album, I will have played my part as spirit and a spirit-person in the symphony of new songs and new stories. So it is, I close with unlimited divine love and unending joy from both of us.

To purchase additional copies of
God's River of Love,
visit our Web site:
www.riverpublications.com

Jacquie and her partner, Jim, moved to northwest Lower Michigan in the fall of 2002. It is a region of great natural beauty, where there are many opportunities for canoeing, kayaking, hiking, backpacking, photographing, painting, and gardening. They are living their lives in this environment as artists of the spirit.